Dawn,

Thanks for your support of KNL and me. May you enjoy many successful Customer Connections!

B. L. Mayfield

What business people are saying about

THE
CUSTOMER
CONNECTION

"The ideas in this book will change how our employees look at our customers and their jobs."

— ART LINKLETTER,
Chairman, Linkletter Enterprises

""This book gives you a practical program to get and keep more customers, get re-sales and referrals, and put your business on the fast track to greater success."

— BRIAN TRACY,
Speaker, Author of *Focal Point*

"A terrific book that's a must-read for every business owner or manager."

— ROGER DAWSON,
Author of *Secrets of Power Negotiating*

"Don't read this book! Don't invest one second of your time, effort or energy turning the pages of **The Customer Connection** *... Unless you want to see your customer and your way of servicing them in a whole new light. This book is filled with practical and usable ideas you and your team will profit from. You'll see the results on your bottom line!"*

— JOEL WELDON,
President, Joel H. Weldon & Associates, Inc.

"A simple story about the simple purpose of business ...focus on the customer."

> — LISA FORD,
> Owner, Ford Group, Inc.

"Want to know how to put Relationship Selling into action? Read this book!"

> — JIM CATHCART,
> Author, *The 8 Competencies of Relationship Selling*

"This is a solid book on a substantive subject pertinent to every company and to each corporate leader."

> — NIDO R. QUBEIN,
> Chairman, Great Harvest Bread Company and
> Founder of the National Speakers Association
> Foundation

*"**The Customer Connection** is a journey through the necessary basics to achieve extraordinary marketing."*

> — KURT HAYDEN,
> Vice President, Sales Manager Kent H. Landsberg
> Company, Inc.

"This is how any company should be structured; around the customer."

> — KEN MARINACE,
> Chief Executive Officer, Comprehensive
> Financial Services

"The book gives a practical knowledge of not only approaching the customer, selling them repeatedly with the best possible service to them but also proving the profits."

> — GIL ROSKY,
> President, Foam Company

"Your book was very easy to read and follow and should help anyone to be able to do a better job of marketing their products to the customer."

— BRAD ENGEMAN,
Sales Rep, STOROpack, Inc.

"To blend customer service, sales and marketing is every companies' purpose. Great read on how to accomplish that."

— NICK ZAMBOLE,
Senior Account Executive, ITA Group

"Terry Mayfield has hit the nail on the head with this awesome book every business person must read!"

— GEORGE HEDLEY,
"Entrepreneur of the Year" Award Winner

"This book mimics our company philosophies to a tee. A must reading for all our employees."

— ROBERT STRATTON,
President, Laser Options

"To blend customer service, sales and marketing is every companies' purpose. Great read on how to accomplish that."

— JEFF GOLDSTEIN,
Vice President, Kent H. Landsberg Company, Inc.

THE CUSTOMER CONNECTION

THE CUSTOMER CONNECTION

A Business Novel that Reveals the Link to Profit and Success

TERRY L. MAYFIELD

MOTIVATIONAL DISCOVERIES PUBLISHING
VALENCIA, CALIFORNIA

THE CUSTOMER CONNECTION

A Business Novel that Reveals the Link to Profit and Success

by Terry L. Mayfield

Published by:
Motivational Discoveries
25852 McBean Parkway #100
Santa Clarita, CA 91355
http://www.TheCustomerConnectionBook.com

Printed in the United States of America

Library of Congress Control Number: 2002101840
Mayfield, Terry L.
    The customer connection: a business novel that reveals
        the link to profit and success/ Terry L. Mayfield.
    ISBN 1-890805-23-8

Book and jacket design by Peri Poloni
Knockout Design, www.knockoutbooks.com

Edited by Karen Stedman

Motivational Discoveries

ACKNOWLEDGEMENTS

We accomplish nothing alone. That's what this book is about. And it came about with the help of many friends and business associates that deserve to be recognized.

In no particular order, I'd like to thank several good friends who helped evaluate the ideas in this book and who helped with many suggestions that improved it immensely.

Fellow Toastmaster **Bob Boog** of Boog Realty. My financial counselor **Ken Marinace**, CLU, CFP^{TM}, RFC, of Comprehensive Financial Services. A superior vendor to me over the years, **Gil Rosky** of the Foam Company. High school counselor **Dan Houghton** and coach on one of the greatest high school football programs ever—Hart High of Newhall, Calif. An excellent businessman with a wonderful sense of humor **Jim Valestrino**, CEO, Los Angeles Label Company. Fellow Toastmaster and entrepreneur **Robert Stratton** of Laser Options. Fellow Toastmaster **Jon Myl**, CPA. Fellow speaker and author of the incredible sales book, *Visionary Selling,* **Barbara Geraghty.** Fellow speaker and humorous fellow **George Hedley** of Hardhat Presentations. Entrepreneur and generous philanthropist **George Schaeffer**, President, Chief Executive Officer, OPI Products, Inc. Founder of an industry and a highly admired business **Arthur V. Geringer**, President, CEO, Security Door Controls. Business associate who treats you like a partner, **Brad Engeman** of STOROpack, Inc. Fellow Toastmaster and quite an adventurer, **Kim Dickens** of Weyerhaeuser Company. Stupendous manager, championship hockey coach, and wonderful neighbor, **Mark Albrent** of Vons Grocery Company. And professional golfer, successful businessman and superior father **Nick Zambole**, Senior Account Executive, ITA Group.

I must set aside three individuals who I've admired and served with in business for most of my career in selling. First, **Bob Werner** who has been a mentor, manager, family counselor and wonderful friend for over 22 years. Bob has been the consummate sales rep whose example and guidance have helped many reps succeed in the area of sales and management. He is the definition of a professional and a wonderful example of a dedicated family man. Thank you, Bob, for all you've done for me.

Second, **Kurt Hayden**, fellow sales rep, philosophical challenger and surf buddy. Kurt, too, is the example of what a real sales rep should be—someone genuinely concerned for the welfare of his customers. He has taught me much about business and life, and makes life's journey fun as well. Thank you, Kurt, for being a special friend.

Third, the numbers king, **Jeff Goldstein**. No one tracks his or her goals and performance more closely than Jeff does. How he predicts what he'll achieve each year is uncanny. Thank you, Jeff, for being my motivational spark in sales and cheerleader for my speaking career.

Although this book is fiction, much of my business experience is the result of working for the most outstanding company founded by **Mr. Kent H. Landsberg** and run by **Gene Shelton**. Their leadership and examples have been invaluable over the years.

My editor, **Karen Stedman** did an outstanding job turning my ideas into a story. I am grateful for all her input, and for being such a delight to work with.

And on a personal note, my father, **Gene Mayfield**, who set me on the right path with his work ethic instilled in me and fills life with laughter for everyone he meets. And my wife, **Stacey**, who put in as much time on this project as I did. I owe her so much in so many ways. I couldn't have a better partner in life.

CHAPTER ONE

I had been at Jensen Printing for 18 years so as you can imagine I had seen a lot of changes. Most of them were related to business growth, and that's what the company had been doing consistently for nearly four decades.

But now changes other than business growth had become a possibility. The company had a new owner. Allen Goodman, our general manager, had just come back from Consolidated's headquarters on the East Coast. Consolidated was the company who'd bought us. They would call the shots from now on. But who exactly were they? And what kind of changes, if any, were they thinking about? That's what the management team and I were expecting to learn at a meeting the Monday afternoon Allen arrived.

Jensen Printing began doing business over 37 years ago. The founder, James P. Jensen, started the company at his kitchen table. He had been a salesman for a medium-sized printing company for several years but wasn't satisfied working there. He wanted to belong to a company built on solid values like integrity, accountability and quality service. Rather than find a company like that, it was easier for him just to create one.

He started working out of his car as a broker selling custom-printed forms and business stationery. Eventually he purchased equipment to do the printing himself and hired people to help him run the shop. In a short time, it became a corporation with more than a 100 employees.

The plan was for Mr. Jensen to retire after 40 years and leave the company to his sons, James Junior and Neil. Junior was the operations manager. Neil was in charge of marketing. But the plan hadn't worked out that way.

The company was sold to new owners, and the sons were out of the picture all together. Now friends and family who worked harmoniously together were wondering what was in store.

After many months of speculation the group was hoping some final answers would be coming from Allen Goodman that would put everyone at ease.

Allen was the last one to enter the conference room. No one spoke as he walked to the head of the table. He plopped his folders down in front of him and forced a smile on his tired face. Allen had come straight from the airport to reveal our fate.

"The news isn't all bad," he began.

That didn't sound very positive, I thought.

"Consolidated's pleased with their purchase. They

aren't sending in any of their own people from the corporate offices. They feel we're doing okay with the team we have now. But..."

The long faces I saw on the others in the room mirrored my own anxiety.

"But, they believe we can improve our rate of growth. They feel we have a greater potential for success. That's why they bought us. They expect to see a substantial return on their investment. The bigger, the better for them; the sooner, the better for us."

"Allen, what aren't we doing now that we should be doing according to Consolidated?" asked Rudy Alarcon, the production manager. Rudy had the most seniority with the company. "We've been successful enough to be purchased by a huge conglomerate. They wouldn't have invested in us if we weren't already headed in the right direction, would they? We weren't a failing company that needed bailing out."

Rudy was concerned about changes that might take place just to make the company look good for the new owners—like new job descriptions for the same jobs or needless shifting of people to and from departments. He only had a year or two left with the company before his retirement. He was the type that preferred things to remain unchanged. He still had the same pencil-thin moustache he had the day he was hired 32 years ago. As far as he was concerned, the company had been going along quite well.

Who could have foreseen that Mr. Jensen would have died when he did? Once the sons gained control all they wanted to do was sell out as quickly as they could. Finally they had.

"Rudy, I understand your concerns," Allen said.

No doubt Allen had some fears of his own.

"But," he continued, "we've been changing ever since the company began. This is just another change we need to work through like all the rest. Consolidated isn't asking us to do anything impossible. They believe in us and they're giving us a chance to do this on our own."

Sales department manager, Dave Hankins asked, "How much time?"

"Time isn't the issue. We need to act now. They feel we can get a much larger share of our existing market and expand the one we already serve. Based on some numbers they showed me from companies similar to ours, I must agree with them. What we need to do to reach the goals set by Consolidated is focus our marketing efforts to identify a larger market and capture more business as well as increase our existing business."

"We've been a sales-driven company all this time, and that won't change a bit if I can help it," Dave asserted. He would have been chewing a cigar right then to relieve some of his nervous tension if the company had allowed smoking. Instead, he twirled his pen like a baton. "We can keep this baby going as long as we remember that sales is what got us here, and sales is what'll keep us growing."

"That won't change a bit. But, we need to look at other ways to create growth. Before we wanted to be number one. Now we have to be.

"It's true. We've been a sales-driven organization. The one area we've been neglecting, though, is how we bring ourselves to market. We've always relied on our customer's growth and referrals to grow our business along with cold calling to companies similar to our existing accounts. We need to get an even larger piece of the pie now, though, and quickly. Consolidated has asked me to submit a marketing plan to them within 90 days to show how we intend to accelerate our growth and expand into other markets."

"Allen, we don't need more marketing. We've got a super sales team now."

Dave sounded agitated at the idea of marketing invading his territory, as if his sales team had been slack.

"Dave, I'm not insinuating that the sales department has been letting us down. It's just that we need to focus our time and energy on growth and expansion more than we ever have before. We've always worked on the premise that your salespeople were to get as many orders as they possibly could, and then it was up to the rest of us to fill those orders. So far that's what we've both done and it's worked. But we need more than an increase in sales from our existing customers. Don't you think we can find ways to improve once we put our minds to it?"

Allen tried to sound like he was asking for Dave's input, but the tone in his voice indicated that a decision had been made. Like it or not, marketing was going to grab the reins and take the lead.

Dave didn't say another word. He simply shrugged his shoulders and slumped into his chair. If it helped his group get more sales, what was the difference anyway? After all, sales is what made Jensen the great company it was as far as he was concerned.

"Dave, sales is the backbone of this company and

it'll continue to be. I give you my word. We're not going to change our direction. We're going to broaden it, that's all."

Allen sounded sincere. After all, he had nearly as many years invested in the company as Dave and had an interest in the company's continued success. But as general manager he was the one responsible to the new owners. And, he needed the loyalty of his employees. He needed them to help create the success he was after. He knew he couldn't do it alone.

"So who's going to be in charge of marketing now that Neil's gone?" Gene Brooke, the warehouse supervisor asked.

"Bob is," Allen said.

My stomach sank. I hadn't been told about that. I thought, "I'm going to be in charge of marketing?"

"And Rudy will take over Junior's position as V.P. of operations."

I looked at Rudy and saw the same look on his face that I'm sure was on mine.

Allen went on to explain a few other personnel changes that would take place, but I hardly heard him. I was too busy thinking about what was ahead. After a few minutes, he concluded the meeting and dismissed us.

So, it was clear: We needed to increase growth— now. And the marketing department would take the lead, with me, Bob Hayden at the helm!

Allen didn't need to ask me in advance; he knew I'd take on any challenge. I figured I was the most qualified by default. I started with the company in the warehouse just a mere 18 years ago. I was a youngster compared to most of the management team. Yet in those 18 years, I had worked in just about every department at the company. Allen probably saw that as an asset. It wouldn't be the first time I had entered new territory; yet, I sensed it was to be the most important move of my career so far.

I ended up staying late at the office that night, packing up my personal things. I found a photo of Mr. Jensen and me at a company party. I wished he were there right then. He always gave you the confidence to do any job, even when you thought you were in over your head. Mr. Jensen knew just how far to let you drift out into the deep end before you got into trouble. Knowing this gave you the courage to go further than you would have on your own.

Carla was staying late, too, moving her things into a new office. She was taking over my old duties as head of the purchasing department.

"Sure glad you took the challenge so I could get the promotion, Bob."

"Not like I had much choice, but I'm glad they took my recommendation to let you to take over for me. Your enthusiasm makes up for your inexperience. Not that you don't know the job."

I wondered why I said that. It wasn't what I meant to say. It was a left-handed compliment at best. Carla was qualified to head the department, and I knew it.

"I know what you mean, Bob. I feel the same way. I don't have the experience that some of the others have, but I know I can pull the team together just as you did. I know I can to get the job done."

It was a relief to hear that. Carla knew what I meant and took no offense.

"I'm sure I'll still need to rely on you, Carla. With Neil gone, I won't be able to go to him for assistance or guidance. I don't know what to expect as marketing manager. I'm going to need all the help I can get."

Carla stacked her boxes to the side giving me plenty of room to get my things out before she took over my old office. I was there less than two years. I never felt I got the time to make all the changes I wanted. My goal was to completely organize the flow of paperwork before I moved on to my next assignment; but it didn't happen.

Over the years, I'd been promoted to positions that came about as the result of the company's growth rather than taking someone else's job.

I'd gone through changes before, but going into marketing was the biggest change yet. I had no concept of what was ahead. I was taking on something new and hadn't a clue what it was about. I began to wonder: Just what was marketing anyway?

CHAPTER TWO

A place was set at the dinner table when I came home. The silence impelled me to call out, "Anyone here?"

I heard a faint voice from upstairs. "Up here, hon. Do you want me to come down and put some dinner on for you?"

"No thanks. I got a bite on the way home. I'll come up there," I shouted as I walked by the stairway to drop my briefcase and coat on the chair in the den. I was too tired to look at the mail on the desk. It could wait until later.

"So how was the big meeting? Are things going to be okay with Consolidated in the picture now?"

Kate's voice was cheerful and optimistic. She was hoping nothing had changed. She liked things to be consistent with no surprises.

I hesitated, then said, "I have a new title: marketing manager."

"Another change?" Her optimism faded. "Why

can't they leave you where you are? You like being head of purchasing, don't you?"

I liked all the positions I had. I'd start working at a particular job by myself, then the company would grow and I'd need help. Once there were two of us it became a department. Someone needed to be in charge, and I was usually labeled supervisor since I was the first one there. After a while the titles grew to manager.

I started out in the warehouse as the receiver, shipper, floor sweeper, whatever. When they hired Randy and Jason to help with the expanding workload, I became the warehouse supervisor. The same thing happened when I moved into the front office. The only exception was when I took over as sales manager after Dave Hankins' heart attack.

He was out for several months. At the time, no one was sure if he'd ever return. Not because of his age; he was only in his mid-50s, but many thought he might try to come back and take a less stressful job. Even though I'd been in sales several years before, I couldn't wait to end my stint as sales manager. So when Dave came back and returned to his prior job, no one was happier than I.

It wasn't that I didn't like being sales manager. The problem was I kept trying to run it the way Dave would have rather than the way I wanted to. I did this with the idea that he'd return soon. I didn't want the sales reps to have to adapt to a new routine and then switch back for Dave. I thought I could have done a fair job if it wasn't a temporary position. But I was trying to do it Dave's way and I wasn't Dave.

After that, I was asked to help organize our purchasing department. I think I enjoyed that job the most. I felt that my experience in all the other departments allowed it to be my proudest achievement yet at Jensen. It was a job that I did get to do my way. It was the first time I stepped into the top position from the start.

The previous manager had retired, so I made permanent changes in the department right away. The department was functioning well, but I was able to make further improvements and bring it up to date mostly with new computer software. Productivity per person was improving monthly. That may have contributed to my being asked to oversee marketing.

"The company is under pressure to expand," I explained to Kate. "We need to do more than increase sales. Consolidated is expecting us to get more of the pie and to figure out how to make the pie bigger. With Neil gone someone had to take over for him. I guess I was their only choice."

"And everyone else's reluctance to take it on," Kate added with exasperation.

She was probably right, but I didn't respond.

"What are Josh and Amy doing?" I was hoping this question would change the subject.

"Amy's supposed to be in her room doing homework, and Josh's at a football workout. He should be home any minute now. As soon as I'm done folding these clothes, I'll meet you downstairs in the family room, okay?"

I began to feel a little hungry, so I went downstairs and looked in the fridge to see what was leftover from dinner. There wasn't much to choose from.

A voice from behind me called out, "Hey Dad. What's up?"

"Josh! Good to see you son. How was football?" Before he could answer I offered, "Want something to eat?"

"No thanks. Football was great. We're still doing wind sprints and stretching to get into shape. We can't run any plays or use pads for another week yet, much less even touch a football. League rules."

I remembered summer workouts. It never seemed much like football without a football.

"So what do you think of your coach?"

It was Josh's freshman year and his first experience with organized sports. He didn't play soccer or little league when he was younger. He was more interested in computers before he got into high school.

"I like him a lot. After tonight's workout he held a meeting in the gym to find out what our expectations are for the year."

"And what did you tell him?" I asked, as if the goal wasn't to win the league title.

"We all said that we wanted to be first in league. But he said that was the goal of the last freshman team, and they only came in second. He told us that this year's goal shouldn't be to win the title."

"Your coach's goal is not to win?"

I wondered what kind of nut they had running the program.

"Not exactly," Josh answered. He was obviously standing up for him, so I decided to keep quiet and listen to what he had to say.

"Coach said that last year's goal was to win. But the team didn't achieve it. He believed it didn't happen because every team's goal is to win. But winning's not a goal. Coach said it's a result. A goal needs to be measurable. The real goal we should be aiming for is to put more points on the board and keep our opponents from scoring. Points can be measured. If we focus on that then the result will be a win."

It sounded different enough to be interesting. I began to listen more intently as Josh continued.

"Coach said that he looked at the stats from last year and determined that if our team had scored just 5 more points on average each game and held the other teams to 3 less points each game, then they would've won the league title.

"He said offense wins games; defense wins championships. We need to improve both if we want a championship. Focusing on scoring and keeping the other team from scoring will make a win automatic. He says it's a cause and effect thing. We can 'cause' more points to happen, and when we do the 'effect' will be a win. Enough wins, and we'll have the title!"

I began to think that Josh was talking about a philosophy teacher rather than a football coach. But what he was saying did make sense.

Josh continued. "Coach went on to say that if we take it even further and concentrate on each play rather than the entire game we'll gain even more control over the outcome. He said our goal on offense this year is to get 4 yards each play. Since we only need 10 yards for a first down, then we should average one every two and a half plays. When we get enough first downs we'll eventually cross the goal line and score. When we score at least three times a game we'll have a shot at winning.

"For defense," Josh went on, "Coach said it's unreasonable to hold any team to zero yards. But, we can keep any team to 2 yards a carry. If they only get 2 yards in four plays it won't add up to 10 yards for a first down. When we keep the other team from getting first downs we'll be keeping them from scoring. Our goal this year is to keep the other team from scoring more than 18 points a game.

"With our 21 points and their 18 points, we'll win every game and the league championship!" Josh was getting more excited.

I was silent thinking about all he had said. "So your goal is not to win. Your goal is to score more points than your opponents. If you score more than your opponents then a win is guaranteed. You want to win. Your focus though is not on winning, but rather on scoring, or, on an even smaller scale, your goal is to gain 4 yards per down. Do I have it right?"

"That's it Dad!" He was pleased that I'd followed his explanation.

"Our desire is to win. With our goal of 4 yards per down for us and only 2 yards per down for the other team we can do it. It isn't realistic to think that we'll score on every play or that we'll keep the other team from scoring at all. But, to keep from getting down when plays don't go the way we want, we need to focus on the thing that's right in front of us—the next play. If we focus on the task at hand and take care of the yardage, then the win should come as a result."

It still was too new of an idea for me to accept without thinking it over more, but I didn't want to stifle Josh's enthusiasm with a lot of questions. So I settled with, "Sounds like you have quite a coach, son. I can't wait to see you on the field in action this season."

"Thanks Dad. I know we're going to win. I can't wait for you to see me out there on the field either."

With that Josh said goodnight and rushed upstairs to share his enthusiasm online with his fellow teammates. I went back upstairs to speak to Amy and ask about her day. After that I headed for the family room to relax with Kate.

Kicking my shoes off and stretching out on the sofa felt good. It was nice to take a moment and appreciate my family and a nice home. Then my thoughts wandered to work.

"So tell me more about this new job of yours," Kate said as she walked into the room and sat on the sofa next to me.

"What about your day?" I asked.

"Not much of anything special. I spent some time with my mom, did some work around the house, read some. Just enjoying my time off."

Kate started working for the school when the kids got older. It gave her the summer off while school was out and it still left her with plenty of time for the kids. And the extra income was nice, too.

"So what about your new job?" she insisted. "What exactly will you be doing?"

"I'm not really sure. I'm taking over for Neil Jensen, but I won't have him around to ask questions about what he did. He and Junior have nothing to do with the company anymore. My guess is that marketing will involve promoting the company and working with sales again."

"Sounds like you'll get to do it your way like most of the other jobs you've had. Shouldn't be a problem for you," she tried to assure me.

"Yeah, but it seems the other jobs were more obvious and well defined, like shipping an order or organizing the warehouse. Marketing seems so ethereal," I moaned. "I don't mean to be pessimistic. I'm just a little puzzled at the moment."

"I'll bet Uncle Phillip would help you."

That idea flashed like a light for a moment. Of course he would. But it never would've occurred to me to go to him for advice. We hadn't talked in a long time—maybe seven or eight years.

"It couldn't hurt," Kate continued. "And I'll bet he'd love to hear from you. Why not?"

"Hum, maybe," was the best I could manage. "I'll think about it. Do you want to catch up on the news? I'll turn on the TV."

I dropped the idea, at least in conversation. I'd have the next day to think about it. At the moment, I just wanted to relax a bit, then go upstairs and fade into bed. Like Josh's coach said, I was going to take it one task at a time.

CHAPTER THREE

As I drove to the office the next morning I thought about yesterday's meeting and my new responsibilities. I wondered what Neil did while he was the marketing manager. I always thought it was more a title that kept him busy and out of everyone else's way more than his workload.

As far as I could tell there was no set marketing plan for me to follow. I wasn't sure where to begin or how to start.

I found myself at the building before I realized it. I pulled into the parking lot and took Neil's designated parking place thinking, why not? I was taking on his responsibilities. I should get his parking space, too.

I decided not to go to my new office that morning. Instead I went straight to the conference room for the weekly Tuesday morning production meeting

Tony Rodriquez, our shipping supervisor, was always the first to arrive. He'd greet everyone as he or she came in and hand out coffee. Instead, he was sitting still, not his usual talkative self. Even Gene was silent, restlessly waiting for the meeting to start rather than reeling off his latest joke. Everyone was there except our fearless leader, Allen.

It was Allen's style to rush in late, more to make an entrance and look important than for any other reason. He'd ask for a quick recap of what had already been discussed, and then add his two-cents worth.

Allen was the last to walk into the room, but he was on time for once. He, too, was feeling some anxiety about the changes that lie ahead.

"Good morning, everyone," he began.

"I've heard some of the rumors about the company's future. Before we begin with our usual meeting let me take a minute and share with you the reality of what's taking place.

"As you know, we no longer work for ourselves. The Jensen brothers sold all shares in the company, including those in the profit sharing program. As I reported to you before, our new owner, Consolidated, intends on leaving us alone for the most part. We're a solid company and they expect us to remain so.

"However, they've showed me what other companies similar to ours are doing in other regions of the country, and they feel there's a great potential here at Jensen Printing.

"We won't be doing any less than before, but they feel, and I agree with them, that we can expand our existing base of customers and capture a larger share of the market. We must maintain the business we have. We must continue the growth we've had, too. But, in addition, we also need to grow into new areas. They didn't buy what we are, they've invested in our potential."

"But Allen, we're already near capacity. The machines can only go so fast."

Brad had a good point. He was the production supervisor. Though he was young and had only been with the company a few years, he knew every machine in the plant better than anyone else. He had a way of getting more out of the machines than they seemed capable of producing. I'd learned to trust Brad despite his youth. He always knew what he was talking about. If Brad said we were near capacity you'd be smart to take his word for it.

"Brad, you're right. But we're not talking about getting more out of the machines than is possible, we're, well, let me put it this way. It's like we have a herd of sheep, and all these years we've been shearing them for the wool and supplying the highest quality wool there is. We're still going to sell wool, only now in addition to shearing, we're going to milk the sheep and sell it, too, for additional value to our customers and additional profits for the company."

Under her breath Naomi whispered, "And milk the employees, too."

"What was that Naomi?"

Allen hadn't heard her exact words, but he knew they were derogatory from the tone of her voice.

Naomi had been the most outspoken one when the sale was announced. It wasn't that she feared for her job—she was ready to retire anyway. But she was like a mother hen to the people she supervised in customer service. She was going to fight to keep things the same. She was probably the one responsible for many of the false rumors circulating in the company, too.

"Mr. Goodman, it was nothing. I just hope that more work comes with more help or more pay or both."

"Naomi, you remember when we bought the Adams Company, don't you?" Allen was an expert at turning an attitude around. His tall, robust stature gave him an imposing presence.

"Of course I do, sir. It was eight and a half years ago."

"And," Allen continued, "during the transition you put in more overtime without pay than anyone else as I recall. I don't remember you complaining then. In fact, you seemed overjoyed with the fact that we'd bought out a competitor.

"Well, this situation is similar, except we haven't bought a competitor. We're the ones that have been bought. Consolidated needs all of us. Any extra work we might have to do will only add to our job security in the long run. To make the acquisition work I need your support on this, Naomi. Are you with me?"

"Of course."

"And the people in your department, will you make sure they're with you and me on this, too?" Allen was shrewd to get her to commit her people. He was really getting her to sell the idea to herself.

"You can count on us, Mr. Goodman. As long as we have jobs and the company remembers us, like they did before, we'll be there with you."

Naomi didn't expect a guarantee from Allen, but at least she expressed her opinion.

Allen knew what she meant about remembering the employees. Only there wouldn't be any shares of company stock to hand out as bonuses like before. He let the discussion end there with no further comment. He answered to the board and shareholders now, not to Mr. Jensen and certainly not to Naomi.

"What all this means," Allen said as he brought the meeting back to his agenda, "is we're going to need to do some things differently. To facilitate this, Bob Hayden has been selected to take over the marketing department. His main task will be to identify areas where we can expand our business. Although you'll all report to the same people as you did before, I want all department heads and workers, to give Bob their full cooperation. Any problems you know of, or opportunities for that matter, too, bring them to Bob's attention immediately. He'll be reporting directly to me.

"As best I can recall, Bob has either worked for each of you, with you, or over you in the past. He's the best person qualified to focus our efforts to increase our market share. Please give him your full support."

He went on to explain the other changes that were taking place, most notably Rudy to manager of operations and Carla's promotion to take over the purchasing management position from me. He didn't go into any more details. He was obviously in a hurry and had other concerns.

"If there aren't any questions," and Allen's expression looked as if he didn't want any, "I won't be available for the rest of the production meeting. I have to prepare for another meeting with Consolidated this afternoon. Nice to see all of you."

With that Allen rushed out. The new manager of operations, Rudy Alarcon, took over.

"Okay, who wants to start with their numbers for

this week? Brad?"

"Brad, are you here with us this morning?"

"Uh, yeah, Rudy. I was just thinking about what Allen said, about us getting more out of what we already have, like the sheep."

"That won't necessarily mean speeding up what we do. There're other ways to increase output," Rudy said, trying to calm Brad's uneasiness.

Rudy decided to have me explain further what Allen had alluded to. So he asked me, "Bob, can you tell us what you'll be doing?"

"Sure," I said, wondering what to say as I stood up.

"As Allen mentioned, I'll be working with each of you regarding marketing. Without going into details now, I'd like you all to know that I'll be getting with each of you soon."

I tried to make it sound like I had a plan, but I really hadn't had the time to figure out what I was going to do.

"I want to find out what projects you've worked on with Neil in the past or any you were working on just before he left.

"That's all I have to say for now."

I wasn't prepared to say anything more. And, that was okay, because everyone wanted to get the meeting over with as soon as possible and get to work. So I nodded to Rudy indicating I was finished talking.

"Sounds good. Let's get this meeting over with quickly. Brad, what orders do you have scheduled to be completed this week?" Rudy said, and the production meeting finally started.

It turned out to be one of the shortest meetings ever.

As we filed out of the meeting I called out, "Brad, Tony, you guys available for lunch today?"

"Sure. Let's meet outside around a quarter to twelve to beat the crowd at The Hut."

"The time sounds good," I said, "but let's go to Presaro's if that's okay?"

I didn't want us to be bothered by other workers that might be there. Presaro's would give us the privacy I wanted. They agreed, and I went to my office looking forward to talking with them later.

Later, as we walked into the restaurant, Tony asked, "Why such a nice place just for lunch, Bob?"

He really meant why such an expensive place?

"I'll pick up the tab, guys," I said, hoping that maybe I could get an expense account since I was almost a vice president. "I just wanted some privacy. I want to know your thoughts about Allen's talk and about any work you've done with Neil lately."

What I needed was their support. Not just as co-workers but as friends.

"You know how I feel," Brad started, "I've wanted to run more complex jobs for a long time now. The machines can't go any faster, but I think I can tweak them to do other types of jobs as well. We wouldn't need much in the way of new machinery, just some attachments or modifications that I can do myself. I'm sure there's a lot more those machines can do than they're doing now."

I hesitated to ask Brad to explain in detail what he was referring to. Tony spoke up before I needed to say anything.

"I don't know about production, but I do know our trucks go out practically full every day. We can't handle more work, at least not without more equipment and manpower."

They were centered on Allen's comment about producing more. I wanted to ask them again about Neil.

"Hey guys, before we go into any details about increasing production, let me ask your help on something else."

I was hesitant to say what I wanted to because it would reveal a fear I had. I hoped they were the right people to say it to.

"They've put me in charge of marketing with the idea that I'll discover a way for us to get a larger share of the market. But I'm not exactly clear on what marketing is. I'm not even sure where to start. Neil didn't leave anything for me to go on. Did either of you work with him on any projects? Do you have any ideas at all that you think could help me?"

Well, I had exposed my fear to them. I'd find out soon enough whether they were good of friends or not.

Tony shook his head. "I never worked with Neil. He never even talked with me other than a hello once in a while. I don't think he even knew my name.

"I can run a warehouse, and schedule and organize all our drivers each day, but marketing is something I know absolutely nothing about. Sorry. If I could I would, but I can't help you there."

"Thanks, Tony. I appreciate your candor.

"What about you, Brad. Did you ever work with Neil?"

"Never."

I didn't get the answers I wanted, but it was close to what I expected.

I looked at Brad and asked, "I heard you went to college and studied business. Do you remember anything about marketing?"

"Yes, I graduated with a business degree. My dad told me it'd give me an edge over others no matter what job I ended up in. I prefer machines to management and theories, though.

"I did take a class in marketing, but I don't recall much about it. What I do remember, though, is that the professor kept emphasizing common myths most people had about what marketing is. He said that most people think of it as another form of selling. As I recall, for our final project he had the class form groups to create fictional companies. As my group worked on its marketing plan it seemed to me that marketing was just about everything a company does."

"Do you still have the textbook?" I asked.

"I don't know," he said. "I'll check and see if it's one I still have."

"I'd appreciate that," I said.

"What about asking for some ideas from our suppliers?" Tony suggested. "You have contacts in purchasing with some pretty big corporations. What if you asked them for some help? If they can help us improve, as we get bigger the more we'll buy from them. They'd like that, don't you think?"

"Good idea," I said. "I'll look into it," and I wrote the idea down in my planner.

"Hey, if any other ideas come to you guys let me know, would you? Brad, you mentioned something about possible improvements to machines. Can you put your ideas down on paper and bring them to me with some specifics?"

"Sure."

"And I've had some ideas I've wanted to try but never seemed to find the time to try them," Tony added. "Do you want those, too?"

"Give me anything you have," I pleaded. "Don't hold back or judge any ideas good or bad. What I need now is input on how we can improve. We can judge later how valid the ideas might be."

As we headed back to the office I was glad I began my interviews with Tony and Brad. I needed to spend more time getting to know them and find out how they could help the company.

After lunch I felt a boost in my confidence to do the job, if only because I had Tony and Brad to support me. I hoped the others would be as supportive and as willing to help. At the same time, though, I realized I was no closer to creating a marketing plan. I wondered where to go from there?

I felt Neil must have left some sort of trail of what he'd done all those years. Or had he really done anything at all? Whatever, I was going to find out.

CHAPTER FOUR

It's hard to find something when you don't know what you're looking for. After spending the better part of the week going through Neil's files, I still couldn't figure out what he'd done as the marketing manager. I'd talked with every manager, supervisor and other employees and still did not learn about any projects he was working on before he left. I did find a new presentation brochure he'd completed a few months earlier for the sales department. On his computer were some spreadsheets charting production and sales numbers. There were other data with no explanation and nothing labeled a marketing plan.

I realized that I wouldn't get any help from what Neil had left behind. I resigned myself to the idea that I'd be starting the project from scratch.

I wished that Consolidated would just let us continue to operate like we had for the past 37 years. I enjoyed facing a challenge, but it was like putting together a puzzle without knowing what it was supposed to look like. None of the pieces were even in front of me. I had to find them first.

I had a meeting scheduled with Allen that morning. I was hoping he'd be sympathetic to what I was facing once I explained my situation to him. He told me when I first took the job that I just needed to pick up where Neil had left off. I was reluctant to tell him I couldn't find the path Neil had been on. At least I had asked to meet with Allen first. It was better than him coming to me and finding out that I hadn't made any progress.

Both of us held several positions throughout the company over the years. Like me, Allen had started near the bottom of the company. I was fairly sure he shared similar feelings that without Mr. Jensen we both could have still been working in a warehouse somewhere.

Allen had been with the company about 11 years when I came aboard. He became Mr. Jensen's "right hand man" shortly after he was hired. He'd been groomed by Mr. Jensen to run the company as a backup should anything happen to him before his sons were able to take over. He even spent several years in sales and enjoyed it and probably would have stayed there, but Mr. Jensen saw his potential and guided his career towards managing the entire company.

Throughout the years Allen had been promoted over several other people who were older and had more seniority because Mr. Jensen believed in ability over time. Allen always came through for him to validate his decisions.

Allen loved the company. His biggest challenge, though, was maintaining his position once the sons came on board. I felt that Neil and Junior never understood how important Allen would be to them in running the company. They seemed to view him as unnecessary once they took control. They didn't appreciate what Allen had gone through that made him such an asset at Jensen.

In the early days of the company everyone did whatever needed to be done. It didn't matter what department you were in. One day you'd be in customer service talking to customers, and the next day you'd receive an order for material in the warehouse. Back then no one cared about who was suppose to do what job. Sure, we each had regular tasks, but everyone was focused on getting orders through the system as fast as he or she could, and taking care of as many customers as possible. Ultimately that was everyone's job.

Now each position was so well defined that people didn't experience the overall mission or purpose of the company. Employees performed well and were dedicated, but sometimes it seemed as though they were more interested in their paycheck on Friday than anything else. And now that the company was sold, morale was lower than ever.

As I walked into Allen's office, though, my spirits were lifted.

"Hi Nancy. Is Allen ready for me yet?" I asked.

"Hi Bob!" she said with a sparkle in her eyes.

Nancy always had a smile in her voice for everyone she spoke to. Mr. Jensen sure knew how to hire people. Allen was lucky she stayed with the company. Many thought she'd leave after Mr. Jensen died. She could have retired years ago but stayed because of her loyalty. Not only did she have over 30 years of experience, she was also a pleasure to work with.

"He's expecting you. Go right on in," she said flashing her usual smile.

I walked through her office toward Allen's, but before I reached his door he was there to greet me.

"Bob, good morning, how are you? How's Kate?"

"Kate's fine. She's off for the summer just enjoying life. Thanks for meeting with me." I thought I might as well get right to the point. I should've asked about his family, but my mind was stuck on the project.

"Let's sit over here so we're more comfortable," he said as he led me to the chairs in the corner of his office near the window.

It used to be Mr. Jensen's office. It was sensible and functional, just like Mr. Jensen. Allen hadn't changed a thing.

It was more comfortable sitting next to each other in the corner. There's something intimidating about talking to someone behind a desk, even if he is a good friend.

"I've been trying to put together our marketing plan and figure out what Neil had been up to. I've talked with almost everyone here at the company to find out if they ever worked on any projects with him. Dave Hankins did, but that was several months ago. If Neil was doing our marketing, I sure can't find out how he was doing it."

"Bob, Neil was more our special projects person than marketing. It was a title. If a temporary project needed to be done, he did it. Seemed sales used him most of the time. He didn't want to be associated with sales so he came up with the title of marketing manager. That was the extent of his job. When I asked you to take over where he'd left off I didn't expect you to find much."

"Well, that confirms that I don't need to look any further."

"We still need to create a marketing plan for Consolidated," he reminded me.

"We'll have one," I assured him.

"Brad Kline in production gave me an old textbook of his on marketing that I'm reading. I'm only part way through it, but I'm getting ideas about how to create a plan. I also did some research online, but you can imagine the thousands of sites I found under marketing. For the most part they're more about selling than anything else. It didn't really give me any direction."

Allen sat still, taking it all in, nodding at times. I think we both had the same emotions of uncertainty. I imagined he was under pressure of his own with Consolidated's expectations of him.

"I talked with Dave about marketing being the same as selling and he agreed. In fact, he seems to think that's all marketing is. He used his usual line that sales are what made this company. As he says, without a sale what's the reason for anyone being here? He does have a point, but do you think that marketing is just selling?"

"Hankins' right," Allen conceded.

I knew he'd see it that way, too, being an ex-salesman himself.

"If nothing gets sold," he went on, "we're out of business. But marketing is also advertising and promoting what we do for our customers and potential customers."

That made me think of something I'd read in Brad's textbook. I hesitated to bring it up with Allen, but decided what the hell.

I blurted out, "That's the question, Allen. Just what do we do? Why are we here? What's the purpose of all of this?"

"Do you really have to ask?" Allen said in a condescending tone. "Excuse the triteness, but the bottom line of what we do here is make money."

He leaned forward in his chair and looked straight at me. "We're in the business to make a profit. And not just for us anymore. We work for the board and shareholders of Consolidated now."

Of course I knew that. I let his statement hang in the air a moment. I had no comeback for it. He was right, and yet it didn't seem to answer the real question. Was money the only goal?

I said the words, but they felt hollow.

"So where do you suggest I start to come up with a marketing plan that'll help us do that better than before? Make money, that is."

He fell back in his chair and looked down at the floor. He gave a deep sigh and said, "Maybe we need some outside help on this. Not that you aren't capable, but my guess is you're like me. We both started here with little, if no business experience. All we know is what Mr. Jensen taught us. Not so much with his words but with his actions. I ask myself almost everyday with practically every decision I have to make, what would Mr. Jensen do if he were faced with this?"

Even our fearless leader had doubts. He was under pressure, too. I was glad, though, that he wasn't making rash decisions like the sons had done when they sold the company.

"You mean hire a consultant to do the job?" I asked. I was hoping I'd get out of the project altogether and return to doing work I knew.

"I don't want to go that route now," Allen said as he looked down again, leaning on his knees with his elbows. "What other sources do we have that we can tap into for help?"

Allen wasn't as much help as I had hoped.

Then I remembered Uncle Phillip. I decided right then that I should see him, but I also thought it'd be wise not to mention it to Allen just yet. I wanted to have something concrete to present later, rather than tell him about it now and raise his expectations. I wanted to be sure I had something of value first. But I felt I needed to share some progress with him no matter how insignificant it seemed.

"Brad and Tony gave me some ideas I'm looking into, but they're only a start for now," I said.

"That's something," Allen said, with little excitement in his voice. "We need to meet once a week so you can keep me up on your progress, and so we make sure and have a plan for Consolidated on time. Check with Nancy to set up a time to meet with me as soon as I get back in town at the end of next week."

We shook hands and I walked out of his office. I left without the help I had hoped for, but at least Allen was aware of the challenge I had.

I walked down the hall back toward my office thinking of the best way to approach Uncle Phillip. It's easier to be humble when you're near desperation. I wasn't quite desperate, but I knew I needed help. My instincts told me I should act now. It was time to make the phone call Kate had suggested a week ago.

CHAPTER FIVE

I drove down the winding driveway, past the luscious green lawn, and parked near the fountain. I got out of my car and stepped onto the cobbled circular court. I wondered how anyone could afford a place like this. I had heard stories about Phillip's house from my sisters, but it was grander than I had pictured.

A woman opened the large, carved wood door to greet me.

"Bob, it's so good to see you," Aunt Patsy said as she gave me a big hug. "You look great. Kate sure is taking good care of you. How are Josh and Amy?"

She led me through the front door and down a long hall toward the back of the house while I told her about my family.

When we reached the double etched-glass doors at the back of the house that led to an expansive patio she said, "Well, we can fill each other in more during lunch. Phil's out back; he's so thrilled that you called him. I hope we start seeing more of you again. Won't we?"

I felt a twinge of guilt when I assured her she would.

Phillip was quite a successful businessman. He started several companies over the years. He even bought a few, including a fledgling one he turned around — the one my father owned when he passed away.

When Dad died I wanted to continue and run the company he'd founded. My sisters felt it was better to let Phillip take it over and have us work for him. I took their lack of confidence as an insult. I also believed Phillip was taking advantage of us, and the situation. In time I came to realize he was looking out for our interests, not his own. I could see later that I didn't have the experience necessary to run the company then. Phillip promised us he'd eventually give the company back to us, but my ego wanted me, not him, to be the hero and continue Dad's success.

So I left the company. My sisters stayed. With Phillip's guidance and business acumen they did exceptionally well. I know Kate must have thought about the different lifestyle that we could have had if I'd only stayed. She's kind enough, though, never to mention it.

When I left the family business I thought I knew so much. I was confident I could get a job easily in management elsewhere, but it turned out the only job I qualified for was working in a warehouse. Without a formal education or years of experience no company was willing to let me start in management. But, I was lucky because eventually I was led to Jensen Printing. I don't think I could have ended up at a better company than Jensen. I was able to gain a tremendous amount of experience and learn about the business world hands on. I know I could have learned the same, probably more, from my uncle, but I let my emotions rule.

As Patsy showed me through the garden I saw Phillip crouched on his hands and knees in front of some roses. Apparently, he still loved gardening.

"Good morning Phillip."

Phillip turned to me with a huge smile and said, "Bob, I'm so glad to see you."

He stood up and brushed himself off. Then he rushed over to me with open arms. No words came to me. As he looked at me with a gentle grin I could see some of my father in his expression.

Patsy brought out some iced tea. She set it on the teak patio table, arranged it neatly, and then left. I sipped my tea drinking in the beauty of Phillip's estate. It was clear that as far as he was concerned, there were no lingering issues between us. He seemed as relaxed as if we'd met every Saturday like that. His calmness put me at ease.

"How are things at Jensen?" he asked, deliberately not mentioning the buyout, which I'm sure he knew about.

"That's why I wanted to meet with you," I said.

I filled him in on what had happened from Mr. Jensen's heart attack to the acquisition. I told him about Consolidated's expectations, and my new position as marketing manager. I finally collected the courage to get to the point of my visit.

"I'd like to ask your advice," I said. "You've been successful at starting and growing companies. You know as much about business as anyone I know. I need to create a marketing plan to submit to Consolidated that outlines how we're going to meet the growth goals they've set for us, but I just don't know how to do it or where to begin."

"I'd love to help you. It's not as hard as you think," Phillip said, smiling as he leaned back in his chair.

Those were the words I was hoping to hear—help and not hard.

"Let's begin with your idea of what marketing is. What's your definition of marketing?"

"What I know of it doesn't seem to be enough."

He said, "Tell me what you do know or even suspect it to be."

"Well," I said, not sure where to begin. "When I think of marketing I think of selling a product, only in an indirect way. Selling is definitely direct. You show someone your product and you either ask him or her to buy it or induce the person in some way to buy it. Marketing, I guess, is like the pre-sell where the customer knows about the product before a salesperson actually sells him on it. Does that make sense?"

"Yes it does," he replied. "Go on."

"It seems that I usually hear the term marketing in conjunction with a product that's been successful, such as, 'they did a great job of marketing it because a lot of people bought it.' So I guess a part of marketing is promoting the product to the customer, either with advertising or public relations.

"It seems a lot of items are never actually 'sold' to people. They just buy them because they're aware of them, like a new potato chip. No one asks you to buy it.

You see the ads, you see it in the store, and you buy it. Marketing gets you to buy it."

"Everything you've said so far is true. What would you say the end result of marketing is?"

"A customer buys the product?" I asked, not sure what he was expecting me to say.

"That's exactly right," Phillip said gleefully. "Most people think marketing is selling, or selling in an indiscrete manner. Yet the end result is just as you've said, a product is bought, whether it's by direct selling or not.

"To help broaden your understanding let me share with you some things marketing isn't.

"Some people think marketing is sales. Some think it's advertising. Others think it has to do with the color and shape of a product or how it's displayed on a shelf. It isn't any one of those things—it's all of them, and more.

"A lot of so-called marketing people are familiar with only one or two aspects of marketing. It's like a child sitting in the driver's seat of a car and saying 'Hey, look at me, I've got hold of the steering wheel, I'm driving a car.'

"Holding the steering wheel is part of driving a car, but not all of it. So is using the gas pedal, knowing how and when to brake, staying on the road, heck, even being on the right road. There's a lot to driving a car successfully. There's a lot more to marketing than most people are aware of.

"That's because there's a lot of misunderstanding and myths about what marketing is. Probably one of the biggest reasons is because most people have been mislead. Are you familiar with the term Multi-Level-

Marketing or MLM?"

"Of course." I recalled the many people who had approached me over the years to sponsor me with what was suppose to be a quick and easy way to make money. "The people who solicit MLM businesses say that you don't have to sell anything, just do marketing. But the more they explain it, it sounds more like selling than anything else."

"That's right," Phillip said. "They try to disguise the fact that selling is involved by calling it marketing.

"People don't want to be seen as salespeople because it's a negative perception. It's the bad, pushy salespeople they've encountered who they remember most. When they do meet a good salesperson that helps them, they don't feel like they've been sold to. They think of it as a purchase.

"Most people think of 'sell' as a four-letter word. Actually, good salespeople use another four-letter word. They don't 'sell' a customer; they 'help' a customer.

"Selling is a part of marketing, but marketing is more than just selling. I believe that most people are confused by what marketing is because of MLM. MLM is not the whole story of marketing. You can call it what you like, but at some point MLM is selling. Through an effort initiated on the seller's part, someone buys something. That's selling no matter what you label it."

So, as I suspected, marketing wasn't just selling. I couldn't wait to share that insight with Dave Hankins. He seemed to insist that marketing and selling were the same.

"Let's try this approach. What about the pen in your pocket?" Phillip asked. "Did you buy the pen, or get it as a gift?"

"I bought it myself," I said.

"Good. Why did you buy the pen?"

"Because I needed one to write with."

"Without going into too many questions about why you bought it, let's just assume you needed a pen for several reasons." Phillip went on, "Where did you buy the pen?"

"At an office supply warehouse type of store," I said.

"Why there?" he asked.

"Because they were the closest store to me. Their prices are competitive, and the service is adequate for what I need."

"Grocery stores sell pens. Why buy it from an office supply warehouse?"

"Grocery stores don't carry this type."

"So the warehouse store had a large selection of pens to choose from, which gave you a better chance of getting the one you wanted." Phillip continued. "What caused you to choose that particular pen?"

"Well," I said, thinking back, "the brand is one I'm familiar with. I assumed that because of the brand that the quality was good. I also liked the style and color of this one, and the price was what I was willing to pay for a pen."

I wasn't a spendthrift, or cheap, but I was interested in getting my money's worth, even for a pen.

"What made you aware of that brand?"

I couldn't exactly recall, but I said, "Probably through advertising in magazines or on TV. I'm sure I knew of other people who'd bought them and they seemed satisfied with them, or at least no one told me not to buy this brand. When I saw it on display I went right to it."

"Were there other brands being displayed?" Phillip asked.

"Sure. Some others I had heard of, some off-brand stuff, too," I said.

"And the brand you chose, was it the only pen from that company that was on display?" Phillip asked, still another obvious question.

"No, they had several," I said. "In fact, once I found the one I liked, the right color, size and feel, I compared it with another brand that had a similar pen. But I chose this one mostly because of its looks and how it felt when I wrote with it."

"So, the appearance and its feel were the deciding factors? Good."

Phillip leaned forward signaling an end to his questions.

"When you bought that pen you completed the company's marketing process."

"I guess so," I said.

"Let's trace the steps the company had to go through to get you to buy their pen.

"First, it—let's say 'they'—had to know you existed —you as a potential customer. Then they had to know that you needed a pen, for whatever purpose. But more importantly they needed to know the features that you wanted in a pen—style, color, a retractable tip, a clip to attach to your shirt and a replaceable ink cartridge, just to name a few. They also knew you wanted a quality pen. A pen you wouldn't need to return and one that would work repeatedly for you in the same way.

"Then they needed you to be aware that their pen

was available to purchase. They did that through advertising and promotions. Even the packaging and display were both designed to focus your attention on their pen.

"They also had to make it convenient for you to buy it. They made it available at a store near you, where other items you might buy along with their pen were, such as paper, folders, staples, binders, whatever. Does this make sense so far?"

"Yeah, it makes sense. Seems like a lot of work just to sell a pen."

"That's it," Phillip beamed. "All the work they went to just to sell you one pen is what's called marketing. Actually, there's even more to marketing once you get into the details, but the process we just described is marketing. Let me break it down for you into its basic steps.

"Marketing focuses on these four areas: *what problem the product solves for its customer, how much to charge for the product, where to make it available to the customer and how to make the customer aware of the product so he or she buys it.* Simply put, marketing centers on product, price, location and promotion—that's what marketing is.

"All marketing begins with the need for a problem to be solved. Without a problem, there's no need for a solution.

"Look at it this way. Remember when personal computers first came out, and they weren't selling as well as companies thought they should?"

"Of course," I said. "I remember people raving about them, but I couldn't figure out why I needed one."

"Precisely. They were a solution, but no one had a problem they solved. People didn't understand what computers could do for them. It wasn't until more and more software came out that computers were able to actually do something useful, such as word processing, spreadsheets or provide entertainment. Then consumers needed to know how they could use them. Once they did, that's when people started to buy PCs."

"It's the old idea that no one wants a drill," I said. "People want a hole, but to get a hole they buy a drill. So marketing is focusing on getting the customer a better hole, right?"

"Right again. The first step in marketing is knowing who needs your product, and why someone would want it."

"So," I presumed, "the first step is to focus on the customer and understand what it is she wants and why she would want it? Seems pretty basic. Almost automatic."

"Basic, yes. Automatic, no. So many products are created and developed without an understanding of who or what they're made for.

"I met a man about 10 years ago who approached me with an idea he wanted me to invest in. He had a machine that was a little smaller than a microwave oven that allowed you to make soda pop and beer in your home for just pennies per glass. He thought he was going to be a millionaire, not just because of the machines he thought he'd sell, but mostly because of the ingredients people would buy from him to make beverages after they had his machine. A great idea perhaps 50 or 75 years ago when people were more accustomed to preparing their own food and beverages, but not 10 years ago.

"What he failed to see was that people don't

necessarily want something cheap. People today want convenience. They go to the grocery store and buy lettuce that's already cut-up in a bag. They pay more for it and could easily buy the lettuce by the head and cut it up themselves, but they pay for the convenience of having it in a bag.

"That man with the soda machine didn't look at who would want his product before he developed it. Again, a good idea, but he didn't understand his customer or consider his potential market. The market for his product, of course, was practically nonexistent. He ignored what people today want—convenience. Making your own beverages certainly isn't as convenient as opening a can.

"The nucleus of any marketing effort, the center of all marketing functions, is the customer. You need to answer who are they, what do they need, what do they want, what do they expect. Nothing else should happen in a company until as much as possible is known about the customer because if the customer doesn't want the product, what's the point of creating it?"

I sat there silent, gazing at my glass of tea, pondering the ideas that Phillip had just discussed. They sort of swirled around in my head wanting to make a connection with several thoughts all at once as I thought about Jensen's products and customers. As simple and basic as his explanation sounded, I could only imagine the implications it would have at Jensen.

"Bob," said Phillip, trying to snap me back to attention, "does that make sense to you?"

"Almost too much sense. I can see where I need to start in order to create a marketing plan—with our customers. I also see I need to consider any company that isn't already a customer of ours, find out how we can meet a want they have and turn them into a customer. We're being asked to make a bigger pie, not just get more of the existing pie. I can see how that type of thinking can help us expand our market."

I put all the ideas in my head together and said, "The customer is the end of the business process when she buys the product. She's also the beginning of the process when a company decides what to sell and why. Everything in between should be completed with the customer in mind. If that's true, then the purpose of a company is to serve a customer."

"Well put," Phillip said.

"Then serving a customer begins even before the customer is aware that she may be one," I continued. "The idea that the goal of a company is to make money is wrong. Making money is the result of successfully serving a customer. Only after a customer is served is there a chance of profit. It's a simple cause and effect formula. The effect, or result, is money. The cause is to serve the customer. Therefore, to be redundant, the real purpose of a company must be to serve a customer."

"Excellent. That's the foundation of marketing."

Phillip leaned closer to me, looked me in the eye, and in a lowered voice said, "I have a task for you. With what you've now discovered, I want you to go back to your company, and with the help of those you work with, decide what it is that each person does that affects the customer. I want you to find out how each individual contributes to serving a customer.

"The task each employee performs is a cause. That cause becomes a result. Everyone at a company must understand how the result he or she is responsible for connects to a customer. Once you've done that then we can talk again and see where to go from there."

All of a sudden Patsy appeared with a large silver tray filled with sandwiches and chips as if she'd been waiting around the corner for us to finish. The three of us spent the next hour chatting and laughing as my past issues with Phillip melted away.

I waved good-bye to them as I drove off. I was glad that I had called Phillip and that we'd finally gotten together again. I was relieved, too, that I had a beginning for creating a marketing plan.

Phillip's insights had turned my project into an adventure. I began to feel excited about my new position at the company. Now, I was even looking forward to the next production meeting and anxious to share with everyone what I'd just discovered — how to fulfill the purpose of our company.

CHAPTER SIX

I walked down the hall toward the conference room. The aroma of brewing coffee told me Tony had arrived early as usual.

I'd just left Rudy's office. I stopped by to ask him if I could be first on the production meeting agenda that morning. Without asking why he said sure. It felt good to be trusted by a co-worker. Rudy was my closest friend at the company.

He was a truck driver when we first met. He made deliveries for Jensen to the company I worked for after I'd quit working with my sisters. Rudy was always saying what a great place Jensen was and encouraged me to go there and fill out an application. I finally went and applied for a job. I owed him a lot for suggesting it. He was right when he said there were plenty of opportunities at Jensen for anyone willing to work hard.

"Good morning Bob," Carla said as she turned the corner in front of me. She had a bounce in her walk. I could tell she was enjoying her new responsibilities as purchasing manager. From what I'd heard, she was doing a great job.

We walked into the conference room together and saw most everyone already there. Several were going over the information they'd be presenting to the group while others chatted about personal stuff. Then Rudy came in.

"Good morning everyone. Nice to see we're all here on time today. Allen won't be here," Rudy added. "He asked that we give some time this morning to Bob's project. As you know, he's our new marketing manager and he'd like our help. Bob?"

Rudy picked up his papers, walked to the other end of the conference table and sat down. I walked to the front of the room.

"Good morning everyone," I began, "and Dave, thanks for the muffins. I know many of us don't get much to eat on the days we come in early for this meeting, and we appreciate sales for providing them."

Dave was very thoughtful of the rest of us. He'd often bring some kind of food for us during the meetings. He always said it was from the entire sales force and not just him. It made up for the rush orders they'd send us on a regular basis.

I started my presentation with the pen analogy that Phillip shared with me the weekend before. It looked like people agreed with me when I concluded that the purpose of our company was to serve our customers.

Dave needed a little extra help with the concept. He was stuck on the idea that our goal was to make money. I tried to make him see we were saying the same thing. Finally, I got him to agree that money was a result, not a cause, and that, yes, we were after a result. He bought into it as long as money was part of the definition. That's why he was in sales. "Money motivates, baby" was his motto when it came to inspiring his sales team. After all, they did work on commission.

"So, knowing that the purpose of our company is to serve a customer, how would you define a customer?" I asked, waiting for replies.

I remembered from a sales training course that immediately after you ask a question you must shut up. You don't want to be the next to talk or you'll end up doing all the talking. I stood there determined to get an answer before I went on. I waited for about a half a minute, but it seemed like half an hour before someone finally spoke.

"Bob," Tony said, "I'm guessing you don't want the obvious answer. A customer is someone who buys from us, right?"

"You're right," I said. "I'm not looking for the obvious. Let me restate the question. What type of person or company buys from us?"

"People who need printed forms, envelopes, brochures?" Naomi asked hoping it was what I was looking for.

"That's the right track," I said. "People who need printed materials are our customers."

"So anyone who doesn't need printed materials is not a customer," Brad added. It seemed that was the first contribution Brad had ever made at one of the meetings outside his perfunctory reports. He wasn't outspoken in a group; he was better with one-on-one social situations.

"Of course," Dave said condescendingly. "Any sales rep knows the first step you take in cold calling is to qualify a prospect. If they don't need what you sell, get the hell out of there and move on to where the money is."

I mentally thanked Dave for his brief course in selling. That wasn't what I was trying to accomplish, though. I continued, ignoring Dave's remark.

"A lot of customers can print their own forms today with so many computers and high-quality printers out there, so just needing forms or printing isn't enough to make them a customer of ours. What else makes a Jensen customer?"

"In that sense," said Carla, "a customer is someone who needs a minimum quantity, requires a certain level of quality within a given budget, and doesn't have the time or resources to do it himself in a cost-effective manner."

"Good, Carla." That was the direction I wanted to go in.

"A customer has to be within our local area," Tony reminded us. "I'm not sending my drivers all over the world to deliver merchandise."

Carla joined in again, "So we provide more than just printed materials if we do all that, which we do. I guess a customer is someone who has all the needs we can meet."

"That's it," I affirmed, glad they were getting in sync with the message I was trying to convey. "A customer is anyone who receives something from us. Doesn't that make sense?"

"Well, not anyone who receives something from

us," Rudy said with a little doubt in his voice. "The bank receives interest from us. Our suppliers receive orders from us. There are a lot of people who receive something from us, but they're not customers."

"Then let's tighten the definition a bit," I said, speaking slowly to get the words just right.

"A customer is anyone who receives what we produce, be it tangible, such as printed materials, or intangible, such as the services we provide. How does that sound?"

They all sat still, pondering what I had said. I couldn't tell if they were trying to agree or come up with an argument. I was questioning it myself trying to decide if it was an accurate statement or not.

Rudy broke the silence with, "It seems to be a fair statement."

He repeated it out loud and slowly, "A customer is anyone who receives what we produce." He waited a moment and then added, "It sounds good to me."

Others were nodding in agreement. I turned and walked to the whiteboard and wrote across the top in large capital letters:

A CUSTOMER IS ANYONE WHO RECEIVES
WHAT WE PRODUCE

I was still thinking about it, though. I could tell the group was, too. I decided it was time to challenge them with Phillip's idea to help them discover their connection to a customer.

"I have an assignment for you," I said. "I'd like each of you to make a list of all the tasks you do. Then I need you to determine what a customer receives as a result of each task you perform. The purpose is to relate each part of your job to a customer. I don't need a lengthy, formal report; handwritten is fine. But I'd like to have it by tomorrow, noon, so I can go over them at lunch. Any questions?"

Brad raised his hand.

"What if some tasks don't relate to a customer?"

"List your tasks first. Then for any you can't connect to a customer leave them blank."

No one had any more questions, so I thanked everyone and turned control of the meeting back to Rudy to continue with the production meeting.

I realized going into the meeting that I was going to ask them to make the list. I didn't know at the time that we'd come up with the definition of a customer that we did. I liked it, though. It made more sense to me than just making money. It reminded me of Josh's football coach changing the goal from winning to scoring points. Maybe we needed to change our goal from making money to helping customers. Surely if we served more customers we'd end up earning more money just as scoring more points in football would lead to more wins.

During the rest of the meeting I found myself thinking back to when I was in sales. At one of the annual sales and awards dinners I got a chance to spend some time with Mr. Jensen, chatting with him about the company, customers, our competitors and some personal talk. It was the most time I'd ever spent with him one on one. I treasured that night ever since, even more now that he was gone.

The thing that stuck with me more than anything else we talked about that night was a statement he'd made about my job. He said that what I did as a salesperson for the company was to bring the company work. He said that the orders I brought in created jobs for eight families. What he was insinuating was that if I didn't bring in orders, eight of the employees wouldn't have jobs. That struck me as rather profound.

For days afterward I kept thinking about what he said. I began to feel that my job was doing more than earning a living for my family. I felt I was actually supporting several families. I began to see it as a greater responsibility. I was serving not only my customers, but also my fellow employees. Mr. Jensen let me see how important I was to the whole company.

I never felt overburdened by the added responsibility, and at the same time I didn't want to become egotistical about it either. But it did make me look at my job in a whole new way.

That's probably what Mr. Jensen intended when he shared that philosophy with me. I began to see a connection with the other people I worked with. I also realized that the work other people did supported my job. They needed me to bring in orders. I needed them to process orders. All the employees at the company were co-dependent on each other for their income.

I imagined that at one time or another he shared that philosophy with other salespeople and probably with managers of the company as well. He was wise in many ways. He was always very business like, yet he engendered great loyalty from his employees because of his genuine compassion and concern for them. He never overtly displayed his emotions, but you always knew he cared.

I was hoping that the exercise I just gave my co-workers would now help them discover the connection of their jobs to customers and help give them a greater sense of how important their positions really were.

As the day went on I kept thinking about what we had discussed that morning, and I became more and more convinced that the purpose of our company was really quite simply to serve a customer.

CHAPTER SEVEN

Dave Hankins had planned to meet with one of his reps in the field, but I convinced him to see me instead. We agreed to meet at lunch.

Dave started with Jensen only a year before I did. Unlike me, he stayed in one department—sales. Mr. Jensen had, in fact, hand picked him to be our sales manager.

Before Dave came on board, he worked for a supplier of ours and made calls on Mr. Jensen. Dave was new in sales then and had no management experience at all, but Mr. Jensen recognized his potential for working with people and convinced him to join the company.

Dave was a people person and much like your typical salesperson—gregarious, fast-talking, friendly. Yet, he was always sincere and genuine, not the backslapping, used car, tell-you-what-I'm-going-to-do type.

Dave was so good with customers that Mr. Jensen made sure he always had several accounts to call on even when he became the manager. Yet he was also just as valuable at motivating the sales team. The only problem with Dave was that he knew and acted like he was great. You can't say he thought he was better than he was, because he was really good. When I first met him it rubbed me the wrong way. But it was easier for me to relate to him after I got to know him better, and later he became a very good friend. He was just a big kid who refused to grow up. Life was one fun game for him.

I arrived at the restaurant first, got seated and ordered. It could be a long wait. Dave could spend 20 minutes in the parking lot on the phone with a customer before remembering he was meeting someone for lunch.

Just as my food was being served Dave burst through the restaurant door scanning the dining room looking for me.

"Hey Bob, how ya doing buddy? Great to see ya. How's the new job going?" he bellowed as he strutted toward me, loud enough for the whole restaurant to hear. "I knew you'd get here first. Sorry I'm late. I had some calls to make in my car before I came in. Customers just can't do a thing without me, you know."

"Hey Dave," I said. There was no need to answer any of his questions. He wasn't asking them to get a reply. It was his way of getting a conversation started. "Thanks for meeting with me on such short notice. Sorry I didn't wait for you to order. Here's a menu."

"The usual salad, huh Bob? No wonder you look so healthy all the time."

After I finished eating and we'd caught up on each other's personal lives, I got down to business after Dave's lunch was served.

"Dave, the reason I wanted to talk with you

today is…"

"If it's about that list you asked us to make yesterday," he interrupted, referring to the task list, "everything I do is for a customer. Do you need me to write it out for you?"

"That's not why we're here, and no. I realize how connected you are to customers so I don't need your list. But that's why I wanted to talk with you.

"You and your sales reps are the closest ones to our customers, no doubt. Going along with a company's purpose of serving a customer, I need to know what our customers think about us. You talk directly with customers everyday. I want to know their perception of what we do. I want to understand their concerns, their needs and their wants. You and your reps are in the best position to get that type of information."

"So what do you want me to do?" asked Dave. "Survey our accounts?"

Yes is what I wanted to say, but I could tell that it wasn't what he wanted to hear.

"Have we ever done any surveys or focus groups of any kind?"

"We tried several years ago, probably when you were still in the warehouse, but it didn't give us any information that helped much."

"Maybe we didn't ask the right questions?"

"Could be. We never tried it again, though," Dave confided. "We've always depended on the sales rep's feedback and on the inside people monitoring and following up on customer complaints. Otherwise, if orders are coming in, well, we don't get concerned. If it's not broke, why fix it has been the attitude."

"And how do you get feedback from the sales reps?" I asked.

"You remember, at a sales meeting. I'll ask the group what's going on in the field," he said. "They'll tell the others things like what orders they've lost and why and what our competitors are up to, nothing formal, mostly commiserating with each other. It's sort of therapeutic. You know how tough it gets out there. We'll support each other to get over it and encourage each other to go out and get more sales despite the problems we face."

"Was any action taken as a result?" I said, with doubt that the answer would be yes.

"If the problem was internal I'd let the department manager know about it. Otherwise, if it was an individual problem I'd work with the rep to see what could be done to get the business back or help with whatever the problem was."

Dave went on. "We listen to our customers each time we call on them; that's our job. Are you saying we aren't paying enough attention to them?"

I assured Dave that I wasn't accusing him or his reps of doing less than outstanding. I did say, though, that I felt that relying only on the rep's feedback was tenuous at best. We needed other ways of getting involved with our customers so we wouldn't miss any opportunities to serve them.

That made sense to Dave, so we agreed to come up with some ideas to focus our attention on our customers' needs. The purpose was not to supplant the sales team, but to find a way to help them and give more support. The point was to increase our growth, which would mean increasing his reps' incomes with more sales.

Dave's response was positive. He was very proud of the fact that they were all high earners by our industry's standards. If there was a way they could earn even more, he was more than willing to help.

We decided that he'd check with some of his larger accounts about how other companies surveyed them and that I'd check with our bigger suppliers and do the same. Surely what we were after had been accomplished by other companies. Why not learn from them if we could?

We finished lunch, and Dave picked up the check as I hoped he would. He did have an expense account, after all. He left quickly to meet with a sales rep. They were going to make a call together on an important customer.

I finished my iced tea before getting up to leave. As I walked past the register I ran into Walter Jensen, our controller.

"Walter, I didn't see you here. I was having lunch with Dave Hankins," I said, startled to see him.

"I know, I saw the two of you in the corner booth," he said.

"Why didn't you join us? We'd have loved your company."

"I'd already ordered and didn't want to be a bother."

How could it have been a bother? Walter was Mr. Jensen's older brother. Seeing him was almost like seeing Mr. Jensen, except Walter was much quieter and reserved.

When Mr. Jensen started his company he worked by himself. He would go out and get orders then go to several different printers to run the jobs. Eventually he bought his own equipment and hired people to run the presses.

He asked Walter to join him after his first year. For the most part, Mr. Jensen did the selling, while Walter handled things in the office. They were originally partners, but when Mr. Jensen wanted to start borrowing money to buy equipment, Walter was too adverse to the risk, so he asked his brother to buy him out. Walter still had a decision-making role, however, and he was the originator of several ideas that had made the company great. Walter continued to work for his brother as an employee. He still worked there now even after the company was sold.

When Walter sold his shares back to his brother he couldn't have realized how much they'd be worth years later. He passed up a fortune. Yet he was never bitter about it. In fact, I suspected he preferred the security of being an employee, rather than the stress of being an owner.

Walter was always pleasant and willing to help out. Rumors had it that it was Walter that kept the company financially stable during the biggest expansion years by handling the company's finances. Without him Mr. Jensen might never have earned as much as he did. If Walter had remained an owner his nephews wouldn't have made the fortunes they did when they sold the company either.

As I spoke to him it dawned on me that I had talked with almost everyone at the company except Walter. Surely, he had some insights for me. He knew more about the company than anyone else.

"Walter, I'm working on the marketing plan for Consolidated, and I'd like your help. Are you available this afternoon to talk with me about it?"

"I'm sorry but I can't. With the sale of the company I have a lot to do right now getting financial documents and information transferred to Consolidated. They'll be handling our financials over at their headquarters soon. After today I'll be out of town until next Wednesday. Can we meet then?"

Disappointed, but glad he'd agreed to meet me I answered, "You bet. I'll get with you when you're back in the office."

With that I left him and rushed to my car remembering I had a meeting with Carla. We were going to go over how she was doing as manager of the purchasing department.

Carla requested the meeting. She wanted to make sure she was doing a good job as my replacement. She asked to meet with me regularly until she felt confident enough to run the department on her own. I thought she had it well under control from the first day she took over. I knew how she felt, though. It would've been nice if Neil had been around to help me transition into my job of marketing. I had a lot of questions but no one to answer them. So partly out of sympathy I was glad to make myself available to help Carla.

As a single mom she was as dedicated to her job as she was to her two kids. Jensen was a good place for her to be. They gave her the flexibility necessary to take care of her family, and she more than made up for it with her loyalty and performance. I could only imagine what little time, if any, she had left to herself at the end of a day. Yet she was always so pleasant. No doubt Carla was an asset to the company. I was glad she was promoted to take over for me.

I sensed that after we met she realized she did have better control of the department than she first thought. I didn't think we needed to meet, but it seemed to boost her confidence. We ended up only spending about 30 minutes together.

Later that day, I read some of Brad's marketing textbook and reviewed the task lists everyone had turned in. I thought I had plenty of time to spare, but then all of a sudden I remembered I was supposed to get home to pick up Kate and Amy by 5:30 p.m. We were going to see Josh's first football game. I couldn't be late for that.

CHAPTER EIGHT

I didn't realize we'd have to park so far away from the game," I said to Kate in frustration.

"I guess they don't have much of a parking lot near the stadium," she replied.

Our son's first football game and we were going to be late. Finally, I found a place to park two blocks away.

"I hope we can still catch the kickoff," I said as we dashed off to the stadium.

Walking up the bleachers Kate said sarcastically, "Well, we made it. And we have great seats."

The stadium was empty.

"Look Dad," Amy pointed out. "There's an empty parking lot right over there."

I wished she'd seen it earlier when I was driving around trying to find a place to park.

"Why aren't there more people here?" she asked.

"It's only the freshman game. They won't have the varsity game until tomorrow night," I said. "That's when most of the students show up."

It was obvious that the only ones in the seats were parents, and few of them at that.

Right as we sat down the visitors kicked off the ball to begin the game. Kate and I were both scanning the field looking for Josh's jersey with number 64 on it.

"I don't see him anywhere. Where could he be?" Kate said.

"There he is!" Amy shouted.

She pointed to a group of players bunched up along the sideline.

"That's him alright," I said realizing he wasn't on the field playing. I still swelled up with pride seeing him in his uniform for the first time with the other boys.

I grabbed Kate's hands as she waved and yelled his name.

"Hon, don't do that, you'll only embarrass him in front of the other guys."

"I want him to know we're here rooting for him," she said.

I spent the next hour and a half explaining the game to her. I was glad she was so interested in the game with her son out there.

Amy was more interested in the cheerleaders and moved to the front row of seats for a closer look. It was fairly certain she'd be out there next year leading the cheers when she was a freshman.

The game ended. Number 64 never appeared on the field during the entire game. I was disappointed. I knew Josh wasn't on the starting lineup, but I hoped he'd get a chance to play at least a little in the fourth quarter.

Kate expressed the same sentiments. I pointed out to her that because the score was so close the coach kept his best players on the field the whole time.

"Well, he still should have gotten a chance to play. He's been practicing so hard," she sighed.

I agreed.

After the game the three of us stood outside the gym, waiting for Josh to shower and change. I wasn't even sure he knew we were there.

"There he is," Kate yelled. "Josh, over here," as she waved her arms.

"Hey guys, thanks for coming. You got to see our first win. Wasn't it great the way we held them on their last possession?"

Josh was as excited as if he had been on the field playing.

"The game went just as we planned."

"Your guys did give me a scare there. I thought the other team was going to score on that last drive, but they held them until the clock ran out. The defense did a great job."

I tried not to let my disappointment show that he wasn't out there for even one play. At least he was on the team and trying. Maybe next game he'd get a chance.

All the way to the car Josh kept going on about the game, and how they stuck to their plan and outplayed the other team, always sounding like he had been on the field and had contributed to the win.

I slipped and said, "Too bad you couldn't have been out on the field to help the team win, son."

"But Dad, I am on the team. The team won, not just the guys on the field." I could tell he was a bit upset with what I'd said.

"I understand what you're saying, Josh. Maybe

next game you'll get to be out there and help the team win," I repeated, thinking he didn't understand me the first time.

"Dad, the coach told us in the locker room that we all won the game, regardless of who got to play on the field. Sure, the guys on the field made the plays, but they needed the rest of us to practice against in order to be prepared for the game.

"Coach made it a point that the guys who didn't play deserved just as much credit for the win as those who did. He said everyone on the team who shows up for practice and for the game counts just as much as anyone else. That's why we're called a team. On or off the field, we all contribute."

Josh began to lecture me. "The running back is the one who crossed the goal line with the ball, but he'd never be able to without the linemen blocking for him. The same is true of the linemen. If they didn't have us to practice against they wouldn't be as prepared for the game as they were. Coach said we could all take pride in the win."

It was obvious that Josh was just as excited over the win regardless of what I'd said.

"You're right," I conceded. "I'm proud of the team, and especially proud of all the effort you've put in. I don't want to take anything away from your victory, son. Great job."

I held back asking if he might get a chance to play next week. I'd just have to wait and see. His mom sure was gloating over him, though. I was glad she came. Maybe she'd overshadow my disappointment. Not that I was disappointed in Josh. I was more disappointed in the coach. I guess I just felt a need to blame someone.

Driving home I naturally started to think about work, and the lists of tasks I'd gotten from everyone. I remembered once that a friend of mine told me about an incident at the company he worked for where management had asked each employee to write out a full description of his or her job. The workers believed it was a way to find out who was contributing and who was expendable in case of a layoff. The result was that people made their jobs sound as important as possible so they wouldn't get laid off. Fortunately, my situation was different, and I was confident that what my co-workers gave me was factual.

When I reviewed the lists I began to see how much each person contributed. There was no one, as far as I could tell, who wasn't doing something to help the company. Obviously there were some workers who had more high-level jobs than others. But, it made me think about what Josh had said—that it was the entire football team that won the game and not just the ones on the field.

I found myself rethinking the importance of every job at Jensen, even if it appeared to be insignificant as it related to a customer. It was like Josh's effort off the field. He contributed to his team's winning the game even though he wasn't on the game field. I was certainly proud of what he'd done. Why shouldn't all employees get credit for helping serve customers? It certainly made me wonder if every employee was getting the recognition he deserved for his or her part in the company's success.

Management was good at recognizing individual efforts from time to time. But did the employees have the same conviction Josh had about their contribution? There needed to be a way to enable employees to see for themselves how they helped serve customers daily. I wondered how to accomplish that. Was there a way for everyone to feel like a part of the team? Josh seemed to have no problem feeling that way and I could see what it had done to his attitude. Wouldn't it be nice if all the people at Jensen felt that good about their job? That stuck with me the rest of the way home.

CHAPTER NINE

Tuesday mornings were nothing to get excited about. For years they began with the weekly production meeting. This time, however, I was actually looking forward to seeing everyone for a change. Marketing was still a puzzle, but I felt I'd put together some pieces. Not enough, though, to see exactly what the finished project was going to be, but something was there already. I was hoping to find some more pieces like I'd found at the previous week's meeting.

I wanted Allen to be there. He'd been traveling to and from the corporate offices so much that we hadn't had a chance to discuss the project.

"Good morning, Tony. Coffee smells great!" I said as I walked into the conference room.

"Thanks, Bob," he replied. "Have you seen Dave yet? He won't be in a very good mood today."

"Why? What's up with him?" I asked.

"He's having a hard time with T.C. Healthcare," he said with some concern. "They're threatening to take their business elsewhere—something about our deliveries, but I'm not aware of any problems we've been having. We're going to talk about it later this morning. I only found out about it when he called late yesterday to confirm what was going to be delivered to them today. He was asking me to get it there at 8:00 a.m. sharp. But if I did that, some other deliveries might not get made, and we'd have even more customers upset."

"So are they getting their merchandise first thing this morning?" I asked.

"They are. I only hope the rest of the orders get delivered on time. It's going to take that driver out of his way to make T.C. his first stop. He's aware of the situation, so he promised he'd do everything he could to hustle the rest of the day and make all of his deliveries. But I can't expect him to work like that every day."

"Let me know how it turns out. I'll get with Dave later to find out what the problem is. Good luck."

By then almost everyone else had come into the meeting room. Dave rushed in with a box of doughnuts and told Tony he'd just dropped off some doughnuts in the shipping office for the drivers. He thanked Tony profusely for getting T.C. out early.

By the time the donuts were passed around the table Rudy appeared, and then Allen rushed in behind him. They filled their coffee cups and joined the rest of us.

"Good morning everyone," Allen began. "Have we started anything yet?"

"Not yet," Carla replied.

"Good. Rudy, you want to get us going?"

It was unusual for Allen not to start with a long speech. He looked tired. The traveling between corporate and home was taking its toll.

"No problem," Rudy said. "But why don't we start with Bob again. I'm a bit anxious to find out how we did on our task lists. Are you ready now?"

"Yes," I said, as I walked to the head of the table.

"Thanks to everyone for handing in your sheets on time. When I asked you to write down your tasks I didn't realize how much you all do."

"Keep those lists for Mr. Goodman when reviews come up," Naomi slipped in, getting a chuckle from everyone.

"And," I continued. I smiled at her, but tried to ignore her remark. "I edited several tasks that seemed redundant. I narrowed the lists down to fewer, more general types of tasks. But I noticed that all of you, except Dave, had quite a few blank spaces where you were supposed to write down what a customer receives as a result of your task. There were more blanks than I expected to see."

Carla raised her hand, and I nodded to her.

"I've got to admit that I went through the list rather quickly, and maybe not as thoroughly as I could have. Where I spent most of my time, though, was thinking about how each task connected to a customer. I had a hard time figuring out what a customer received as a result of what I did. I really did try."

The rest of the group nodded in agreement with her as if they'd experienced the same thing.

"Let's take a look at your list, Carla, and see what we can come up with as a group," I said.

I glanced at her column of tasks. She seemed to have covered all the responsibilities of a purchasing manager.

"The first task you list is quoting suppliers for the

best costs and availability of materials. You've indicated that this results in lower prices for the customer. That makes sense.

"Then you listed entering the description of the material on a purchase order."

"That's one where I didn't see a connection to a customer," Carla said. "The customer's not aware of all the details, probably doesn't even care about the specifications of my purchase order. It matters to us, though, and the supplier, but not a customer."

"But our receiving department is concerned about the details," Rudy interjected. "They need detailed information so they know that what they receive is correct. It's their job to inspect everything and match it up to the correct order in house. Otherwise, the customer may get the wrong order."

Brad's voice came from the back of the room, "So maybe the receiving department is Carla's customer if they benefit from the details on her P.O. The customer gets the right order. So, the benefit to the customer is indirect. The benefit to receiving is direct."

The room was completely silent. Everyone was deep in thought.

I interrupted the quiet.

"Let's look at another line you've left blank. 'Follow up on late orders not yet received.' Doesn't that affect a customer? If we get the materials in late, doesn't it delay the delivery of her order?"

"Not necessarily," Carla replied. "That's why I left it blank. Even if we get the material late, which is not unusual, Brad can sometimes shift jobs around to make sure it still goes out on time. The customer's order isn't affected. The customer would have no way of knowing that a delay ever happened."

"So I'm the one who benefits from expediting an order," Brad said. "When you follow up on an order and make sure that it gets here on time, then I don't have to shuffle production around and hustle the machinists to meet delivery dates at the last minute."

Then Tony spoke up. "That's why I left some blanks, too. Even though many of the tasks in shipping result in serving a customer, a large number of them really serve someone here at the company. Turning in the delivery receipts at night is an example. By then the customers already have their stuff, but the billing department needs the receipts in order to invoice customers."

"Good point," I said. "But if billing doesn't get the receipts from you, then the customers won't get billed. As much as they might want it free, they still need invoices to clear up their books. It still becomes a result for customers."

"If that's the case," Brad added, "then everything we do is for a customer, at least indirectly. I make sure the machines are set up so the orders are run correctly. Customers never know who I am, just as I never really know them. They expect their order to be correct and on time. They take it for granted. I guess I take it for granted that they'll place orders with us."

Brad was getting to the crux of what we were after. Some people looked puzzled, so I decided it was time to sum up where we were.

"Very insightful Brad," I said. "Let me ask everyone here, based on the list of tasks you created, is there anything on them that couldn't be indirectly related to a customer in some way?"

I handed their lists back to them. Several started writing on the blank side of their sheet.

After a few minutes, I said, "Let me ask again, now that you've reviewed your lists, is there anyone who has a task that isn't at least indirectly connected to a customer?"

No one spoke.

"So, I can assume, then, that everything you do affects a customer in one way or another?"

They all nodded in agreement.

"Of those things that have an indirect effect on a customer, do they have a direct affect on someone within our company?"

Again they reviewed their lists. Then Naomi raised her hand.

"It seems I have several tasks that have a direct effect on customers since I deal with them on the phone. The things on my list that are indirect for a customer, though, are a direct result for someone here at the company."

She paused for a moment then said, "Hmm, I never thought of it that way. Using the definition that a customer is someone who receives what I produce, then there are customers within the company. I guess other workers here are my customer, too."

I found myself thinking of what Mr. Jensen said to me about my job — that I was responsible for eight other workers. We're in the business to serve customers, and at the same time, we're also serving each other at the company.

I also recalled what Josh's coach was teaching the football team. Not every player performs on the field in front of the crowd. It's the same with some employees.

They have tasks that customers never actually see, like Brad running the machines or Josh running plays at practice. But, the coach made every team member aware that his effort off the field and away from the crowd *did* have an effect on what the crowd saw during a game. Their impact is so significant that even those who weren't on the field deserved cheers from the crowd.

My thoughts refocused on the meeting, with everyone looking at me, waiting for me to continue.

"So," I said, "our job is to serve a customer. A customer is someone who receives what we produce. But it appears that we have two types of customers—external and internal."

"Does that mean," Carla asked, "that we should treat both customers the same?"

"Why not?" Rudy said. "I wouldn't mind being treated like a customer from the people I receive work from. Who wouldn't appreciate consideration and respect? Not that I don't get it, but maybe I should think about how I'm treating my internal customers because the result will be felt by the external ones eventually. If someone does his job slovenly, how is the next worker supposed to pass it on in any better shape than he received it? Eventually everything we do ends up with an external customer, right?"

The room started buzzing with everyone adding to what Naomi and Rudy had already said, mostly affirming the same sentiments.

I let the discussion continue for several minutes. The mood in the room was up.

"Okay, let's come back as a group," I had to shout

over the noise.

"Here's what we need to do next. I want you to list all your internal customers and determine how they need what you do in order for them to do their job. I don't think it should take you too long. Please get them back to me by tomorrow, noon. Any questions?"

No hands went up.

"Good. If you need any help see me after the meeting."

I grabbed my papers and left the front of the room as Rudy took over the production part of the meeting.

Allen, who had been quietly observing all that had gone on, walked up behind me and tapped me on the shoulder. He motioned for me to go outside with him.

As soon as the door closed behind us he turned to me and said, "Where did you come up with that exercise?"

I just looked at him. It wasn't anything that I'd planned, or expected.

Luckily before I answered he said, "I was sitting there mentally listing all the things I do. It occurred to me that what I do—give directions, manage people, set policy, provide support and motivation—all those things are what the workers receive from me. The entire company is my customer. I'm not over them; I'm under them. I serve them."

I remained silent.

"Bob, when you get everyone's list I want you to map it out as quickly as you can. Meet me Thursday morning to go over it."

Just as he was about to enter his office, he looked back at me and added, "You'll have my list by noon tomorrow, too," and left me standing alone in the hall.

It was time to visit Uncle Phillip again.

CHAPTER TEN

I was glad that Phillip was able to see me on such short notice and in the middle of the week. Even though he was semi-retired it was difficult to catch him at home. He and Aunt Patsy traveled a lot. I didn't think I'd need to see him again so soon. In fact, I was a little embarrassed. I wanted to complete my project by myself, but I felt I had reached an impasse. But at this point, my pride wasn't important. The deadline for submitting the marketing plan was getting near.

I rang the doorbell and a strange man answered it.

"Good evening Mr. Hayden. Please come in."

I was surprised to see that Phillip had a butler.

"Your uncle will be meeting you in his den," he said. "Please follow me."

He led me down a long hallway. Then we passed through a set of large double doors into a library. The ceiling must have been 12 feet high. One wall was covered with shelves of books from floor to ceiling. The far wall was decorated with etched, pane glass with French doors leading to the patio we had lunch on. The gentleman told me to make myself comfortable and that Phillip would be with me shortly.

I explored the room amazed at the number of books and wondered how many of them had actually been read. Another wall was covered with photographs. I was looking to see if there were any with me in them when Phillip walked into the room from a hidden door in the corner.

"Welcome Bob. Good to see you again. You, your dad and I are in that bottom photo there. It's a fishing trip we took in the Sierras."

"I don't remember a fishing trip. Who went?" I asked. I looked pretty young in the picture.

"I stayed at a cabin for a week with some business partners. You and your dad came by for the weekend. It rained the whole time. We never did get a chance to go fishing. You were quite bored having to stay inside the entire time with a bunch of old men playing cards all day."

"That's probably why I forgot about it," I said smiling.

"So," Phillip jumped right to business, "what's happening with your marketing plan?"

He walked over to a chair near a large antique desk and sat down. I followed him and sat in a large leather chair next to him.

"Well, we went through the exercise where the employees identified how their job connected to a customer."

"Were they able to see that they had internal customers as well as external?" he asked.

"They did," I said. "Everyone realized that other

employees were their internal customers. Then they matched their tasks to them. Next we're going to map their jobs out on paper to see how each task eventually contributes to meeting an external customer's need."

"What was their reaction?" he asked.

"They seemed quite surprised. Even Allen, our general manager, was interested. I didn't ask him for a list of his tasks—he volunteered to do it. He was impressed with the idea and was anxious to see the results."

"You understand, it's only a start," said Phillip. "The main idea is for them to be thinking about the customer. Once they buy into the idea that serving a customer is their only job, be it direct or indirect, then it makes the entire concept of how a company runs easier to understand. After they accept that concept, then they can go on and learn the formula. Then it'll make sense to them."

"What formula?" I asked. That was the first time I'd heard him mention a formula.

"The formula for a successful company. Let me write it out for you."

He reached into a desk drawer and took out a pad of paper and grabbed a pen from the desktop. He wrote:

$$(CW \times S) - E = P.$$

"Didn't we talk about this last time?"

"No we didn't," I said. "I'm sure I would have remembered. What does it mean?"

"The result that any entrepreneur, shareholder, CEO or business owner is after is profit. That's what the **P** stands for.

"But, before you get a result you need to have a cause. The cause is the satisfaction of the customer. That's the purpose of any company—to serve and satisfy a customer. A company creates a product or provides a service for one reason—to meet a customer's want. The **C** stands for Customer or Customers. The **W** is their Want. The **S** is Satisfaction, or how satisfied they are by the way their want is met. The multiplication sign between the Customer Want and Satisfaction is there because the degree of the customer's satisfaction will vary. You can satisfy a large number of wants a little, or you can satisfy a single want in a tremendous way.

"Once customers are satisfied, meaning they have received what they want and have paid you for it, then a company's expenses—that's the **E**—are subtracted. What's left, if anything, is profit. Customer Wants multiplied by Customer's Satisfaction, minus all Expenses equals Profit. Profit, of course, can be a negative number if the expenses are greater than what the customer's satisfaction is.

"Easier said than understood," I concluded.

"It'll sink in," Phillip said. "Let me expand on it a bit to help you.

"First, let me explain the difference between what customers need and what they want. Pay close attention."

"People buy what they want, not what they need. Let me say that again. People buy what they want, not what they need.

"Take cars. Almost everyone needs transportation, right?"

"Of course. Especially in this city," I said.

"But, look at the variety of cars people buy. They buy the car they want to own not the one they need. What's the color of your car?"

"Green."

"Did you choose green, or was it the only color they had?"

"I would have taken silver, but they had the green I wanted."

"See. You wanted green. And how much does the color affect the performance of the car?"

"Not at all," I said, realizing what he was getting at.

"It's a fine line between want and need," Phillip said, "I don't want to get to caught up in semantics, but for the most part the emphasis needs to be put on the want."

"That makes sense. That's Selling 101," I said.

"You're right, it is. It's as basic as can be. Your company must focus on what its customers want. Nobody needs your printed forms. What they want is to organize information so it's easily communicated between people. Look at it this way."

He turned to a blank page of paper and drew a long horizontal line centered over a triangle. It looked like a teeter-totter.

"Imagine this long plank resting on what's called a fulcrum. It's one of the five basic machines of ancient times. The plank, when placed on a fulcrum, acts as a lever."

"The right side of the plank points to a scale. At the bottom of the scale is zero dollars, and as it rises the dollars increase. This represents profit."

Phillip drew dollar signs to the right of the plank.

"The point of the fulcrum is in the middle of the plank for now. To the right of the fulcrum, resting on the plank, are expenses. The more expenses you add to the right side the lower the plank will be, pointing to less and less profits. The more the expenses are reduced, the lighter the right side will be. With the right side lighter it makes it easier to lower the left side. When the left side goes down, the right side goes up and points to increased profits.

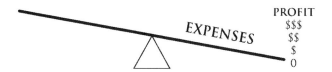

"But here's the rub. The fulcrum is never in the middle of the plank. It can never be closer to the middle than 49% from the left."

"That's because," I interrupted, "even if expenses were zero, which they can never be, the plank would still tip down to zero profit as long as there is nothing on the left side of the plank."

"You've already got it," Phillip said with a smile. "Can you finish the explanation?"

"I'll try," I said. "On the left side of the plank are customer wants. The more wants you place on the left side of the plank the heavier it becomes. As the left side lowers, the right side rises overcoming the weight of expenses and points to increased profits."

"You've got it! Rather simple isn't it?" he asked.

"Yes it is," I said. "The more customer wants you fill, and the less expenses you spend to fill them, the greater the profits will be. But is the fulcrum always one degree to the left of center? Is there anything that would cause it to move farther to the left?"

"Yes," Phillip said emphatically. "When you start out in business the fulcrum is far to the left, which makes it harder to move the left side down and the right side up. For most businesses it stays there. They never learn how to move the fulcrum closer to the center and make raising the right side easier. They don't understand how to leverage their business to increase profits.

"By meeting a customer's want, pressure is added to the left side of the plank, but not necessarily enough to raise the right side and show any profits.

"Since expenses will never be zero there is always some pressure on the right side to overcome. Moving the fulcrum closer to the center is the goal every company should be reaching for.

"The fulcrum slides left to right on a scale based on customer service."

He drew a line under the fulcrum and labeled it service.

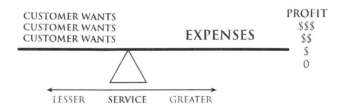

CUSTOMER WANTS		PROFIT
CUSTOMER WANTS	EXPENSES	$$$
CUSTOMER WANTS		$$
		$
		0

LESSER   SERVICE   GREATER

"To the left is less service, to the right is greater service. The level of service the customer perceives determines where the fulcrum is in relationship to the plank."

"So," I said, "the way to raise the right side of the plank and point to increased profits, is to either pour on a lot of customer wants on the left or give better service and move the fulcrum toward the center.

"It would seem obvious that the best way to increase profit is to meet as large a number of customer wants as possible and at the same time increase the level of service. That way you have a lot of weight pushing down on the left side, and with the fulcrum near the center it's easier to raise the right side and increase profits."

"Congratulations. You've got the formula for success in business," Phillip said as he reached out to shake my hand.

I looked at his drawing and let all he had said sink in. I repeatedly flipped to the page with the formula on it back to the page with the drawing.

"Does it make sense, Bob?"

"It does," I confessed. "It fits in with the idea that the purpose of a business is to serve a customer and that only after they are served is there a chance of any profit."

I flashed back to Josh when he first told me about his coach's philosophy about their goal not to win, but to score points. I could visualize the same drawing for football. Instead of Customer Wants the left side would be stacked with 4-Yard-Gains. The expenses to overcome on the right side would be the points scored by the other team. As long as they put more 4-Yard-Gains on the left than points scored on the right the scale would point to a win. The customer service scale below the fulcrum would be the same as the amount of effort the players put into the game — greater or less — that determined where the fulcrum was positioned under the plank.

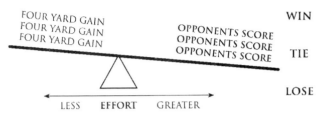

In a sense, it's a company's goal to score points with customers by meeting wants and doing it in such a way that satisfies a customer.

"Bob, you're familiar with the phrase that you never get a second chance to make a first impression with a customer?"

I nodded my head yes.

"It's true, but I don't think people continue to judge a company, or people for that matter, based on their first impression — they judge them on their *last* impression.

"Have you ever done business with a company for a long period of time because things always went well, until something didn't go right?"

"Of course," I said. "I hate to say but I've changed cleaners so many times, I can't even remember them all."

"And you probably went to each of them more than once before you switched, right?"

"Yes," I admitted. "I even went to one I liked for almost a year before they started messing up. I was surprised. I thought for sure that I'd found a good cleaners that I could stay with. But they let me down, too, like all the rest."

"See. That's what I mean," said Phillip. "Your first impression only lasted until you formed another one. Something eventually happened that erased your first good impression and replaced it with a bad one.

"You're only as good as what you've done for the customer lately. A good first impression is fine, but a bad last impression brews in the mind of the customer for a long time. That's why it's so important to continuously monitor what the customer thinks of you and how you're doing. If you don't ask, most customers won't tell. And, it's not enough just to ask. You need to really find out if you're meeting his or her wants.

"I'm curious," said Phillip, "Did you give that cleaners a chance to fix whatever problem they had, or did you just quit going back to them?"

A bit ashamed I said, "I put up with the problem for a while, hoping it would go away. But, it didn't, so I quit going to them. I guess I should have brought it to their attention, but I didn't."

"See, they never even had a chance to fix it," Phillip said. "You shouldn't have had to bring it to their attention. It was their responsibility to find out what you thought about their service."

Trying to explain myself further I said, "The cleaners before them kept breaking the buttons on my shirts. I pointed it out to them several times, but they never changed and continued to break the buttons, so I went to another cleaners.

"When I had a problem with the next cleaners, I thought why bother saying anything. The previous place didn't do anything when I pointed out a problem. I felt I'd probably get the same reaction from the new cleaners."

"I've done the same thing," Phillip said. "I went to a new restaurant this last Tuesday. I was in a hurry and dropped in for a quick lunch.

"The food was so-so, but the service was terrible. Even though I told the waiter I was in a hurry I ended up waiting 10 minutes for the check after I'd finished eating.

"While I was waiting for the change the manager, or at least I took him to be the manager, stopped by with a big smile and asked, 'Is everything all right?'

"I didn't want to take the time and explain to him all that was wrong. I also didn't want to start a confrontation, partly because I wasn't convinced that he really cared. So I simply said everything was fine.

"When I left the manager must have thought I was satisfied and that I'd return. I was thinking I'd never come back here again. Should I have told him? I don't think it's my responsibility to let him know what's wrong with his business. I believe it's his job to find out, not just ask if everything's okay."

I knew exactly what Phillip was talking about. I've done that sort of thing many times before. It made me wonder if Jensen customers had ever done that, too. Of course they had. Why would they be any different than Phillip or me?

"That's why," Phillip said, going back to his illustration, "a company needs to know what its customers' wants are and what their expectations are. It's the customers' perception that is important, not the company's. The company must find out what the customer thinks. The more wants you satisfy, the more you can leverage your profits.

"Until a company knows what wants its customers

have, what wants they are fulfilling and what wants they aren't fulfilling, the company only has, at best, a lucky shot at satisfying a customer."

"So asking the customer if everything is okay isn't the way to do it, what else can be done?" I asked.

"Have you heard of the term SWOT Analysis?"

"No," I confessed.

"A good marketing plan or business plan has a SWOT Analysis in it. SWOT stands for Strengths, Weaknesses, Opportunities and Threats.

"Most businesses sit around a table and try to decide what strengths, weaknesses, opportunities and threats they have. What they need to do is turn those into questions and ask their customers what they think, since they're the ones who ultimately decide a company's success or failure."

"But, going back to your restaurant experience, didn't the manager ask you what you wanted?" I asked.

"No," Phillip quickly replied. "He asked me if everything was all right."

"And you lied and said it was all right," I said.

"That's not true. As far as I was concerned I was going to be getting my change back any moment. I'd be rushing out of his restaurant as quickly as I could, and never walk in it again. Based on that, as soon as I got the hell out of there everything would be all right. "

"But you didn't tell him what you were thinking," I pursued.

"He didn't ask me what I was thinking."

"And you didn't tell him what you were thinking."

"Why should I? If he wanted to know what I was thinking he should have asked me."

"How should he have asked you?"

"With an open-ended question."

"What do you mean by that?" I asked.

"He asked a close-ended question, which only requires a yes, no or maybe for an answer. Such as, are you cold? Yes. Did you go to the game? No. Is everything all right? Yes."

"So," I wondered, "how should he have asked you? 'What are you thinking?'"

"Well, as we agreed, you won't find out bad news from a customer by waiting for him to offer it to you. Most people don't offer that information. It's the rare customer who'll actually say something. If a customer does complain you can be pretty sure there are several other customers who've had a similar experience but didn't speak up.

"The answer is through the SWOT Analysis. There are three questions that must be answered. The key is to ask them in a way that requires the customer to respond with more than a yes or no.

"The *first* question deals with the strength part of SWOT. You simply ask the customer, 'What have we done for you that you like?'

"That type of question can't be answered with a yes or no. The customer has to think and put an answer into his or her own words. It's designed to get more information than 'Is everything okay?'

"That question starts the interview on a positive note. There must be something they like about your company or product. It also tells you what you're doing right so that you can keep on doing it. What a customer likes may be some incidental service you offer. You may assume that no one pays attention to it and discontinue it someday. However, that action may cause a problem for some of your customers. If you don't know what your strengths are how will you know to continue them? When you find out from a customer what your strengths are, then you need to make certain they remain strengths.

"The *second* question is difficult and takes a lot of courage to ask. You need to ask the customer 'What have we done that you don't like?'

"Someone might say you're taking a risk by asking such a loaded question. Why bring up problems that may have already been resolved? Actually, it's a bigger risk to not know what problems are on the minds of your customers. This deals with the weakness part of SWOT. If you don't know what your weaknesses are how will you ever be able to diminish or eliminate them? Even if a customer says there aren't any, don't just sigh in relief and let it go at that. Pursue, dig, probe—it's the only way to find out what a customer really thinks about you. Of course, paying close attention to complaints, no matter how small they may seem to you, is another way of locating weaknesses. Listen to your customers, especially when they have a problem. Be glad when they take their time to share it with you. Better they share it with you than with other potential customers. You can help solve the problem, but only if you know about it.

"The *final* question you need to ask a customer is, 'What could we do to improve our service or products for you?' This, of course, deals with the opportunities of SWOT. I've gotten more great ideas from customers with this question than any brainstorming session I've ever attended. Customers are in a unique position. They know what they need and want; for us it's only a guess. Cultivate your customers for ideas on how to improve, and they'll come through. Asking them makes the customer feel like part of the system. They feel like they have a say in what happens; and they should.

"If you ask these three questions of your customers you'll have more than enough information to add wants to the left side of the plank and increase your service to them."

"So what specifically should that restaurant manager have said?" I asked.

"Well, he could have started with, 'Thanks for coming to our new restaurant. What have you enjoyed about your visit so far? Was there anything that didn't meet your expectations?' Then, 'what can we do to improve your next visit?'"

I thought a moment, then asked, "But that's only three questions. What about the threat part of the SWOT? How do you discover your threats?"

"A company faces many threats," Phillip said. "Some are competition, the economy, rising interest rates, regulations, weather and more. A company, though, has little if any control over these. You must be aware of them and you must deal with them. But the two biggest threats to a company's survival are, first, not asking customers the three questions, and second, not acting on the information once they have it. The better you know what your customers' wants and expectations are the more you'll be able to leverage profits."

I sat back in the soft leather chair and viewed the

opulence that surrounded me. Phillip must have known what he was talking about. It was such simple stuff, yet it made so much sense.

Phillip stood up, looked at his watch and said, "I think that should give you something to work on for a while."

That was an understatement. I got the feeling that the marketing plan was getting larger than I ever thought possible. The more I uncovered, the more there was still to discover. I had a hunch I needed to learn more about our customers. Now I knew how.

I thanked Phillip for sharing his time with me again. I also asked him if he and Patsy would come over for dinner soon and see Kate and the kids. He said he would love to. I promised to get back to him after I talked with Kate about when would be a good time to get together.

As I left, I grabbed the notepad with the formula and the plank and fulcrum drawing on it. I wanted to take it back to work with me. Then I thought to write down the SWOT terms and the three questions. I didn't think I'd forget the concepts, but I wasn't going to take any chances.

Phillip walked me out to my car and hugged me. It made me think of Dad. Not that he and I hugged much. I couldn't remember a time as an adult that we had. Being with Phillip somehow stirred up some old memories and made me wish I could hug Dad again.

Driving home I thought of all that had happened to me in the last few weeks. My life was going in a new direction. I had a new position at the company and a different view of it than before. And, I had rekindled my relationship with my uncle, which I thought would never happen. I wondered what would be next?

I decided I'd had enough change for the time being. I just wanted to get the marketing plan completed. I'd figure out what was next once the plan was in writing. At the moment, I needed to get ready for another meeting with Allen so I could tell him what I had discovered. I had even more to share with him than I had expected. Kate was right when she suggested I see Phillip. I was glad I listened.

CHAPTER ELEVEN

No two days were the same. Each day I felt like I was walking through a black door into the unknown.

Allen cancelled our next meeting, which was fine with me. I needed a break. I decided to use the time instead to check with Dave and find out what was up with T.C. Healthcare. He told me he had a meeting scheduled later that morning with the buyer at T.C. He was going to find out why there was a problem with our deliveries all of a sudden. They'd been a customer for years. It was unusual for them to have a complaint. I asked him if I could come along, and he said okay since the sales rep for the account was out of town.

Dave told me it would probably be better that our sales rep wasn't able to go. Sometimes, he said, customers won't want to share anything negative with a salesperson for fear that it will sound like the sales rep's not doing a good job. Buyers tend to see their sales rep as a friend and don't want to get him or her in trouble.

Dave now hoped the customer would be more open about how he felt about our company. And, he said, if the problem turned out to be the sales rep, it would be better if she weren't there to allow the customer to express himself more freely.

Dave said he'd meet me in our lobby at 10:30 a.m. It was a good thing I keep a suit jacket in my office. I hadn't worn one in months. I knew, though, I better look sharp for the customer.

Dave was running late as usual so I found myself sitting alone in our lobby. I began to wonder what customers must think when they're here. It looked clean, neat, and the chairs were comfortable enough.

Then I looked down and noticed the magazines on the table. There were several rather old copies of ones about famous people, an old industrial advertisement for a mail-order company and a dated business journal. What message did that give to visitors about our company?

The walls were rather stark with only a few cheap paintings, and our mission statement hung by the door. Other than that, it could have been the lobby to a dentist's office or an accounting firm.

Without warning Dave burst through the door, spewing directions to the receptionist as to where he would be, when he'd be back, whom to forward calls to and whom to take messages from. I couldn't imagine she retained anything he said.

"Hey, Bob, let's get going. I hope the traffic's not bad."

I jumped up and practically ran to keep up as Dave rushed out to the parking lot to his car.

He cleared the front seat off for me tossing files and

papers into the trunk. He drove a nice car, but it was hard to notice through the clutter. It looked like he lived in it with so much stuff everywhere.

"I think we can get there on time," he said, panting as if running out of breath. "It should only take about half an hour. I'll wait until we're almost there before I call to tell him we might be late."

In between sharp turns and frantic lane changes I told Dave about my evening with Uncle Phillip. Dave was pretty quiet, barely nodding his head from time to time. I thought he'd have more to say, but he was probably concentrating on the traffic and what lie ahead for him at T.C. It was a big account for the company, and it was his responsibility to make sure it stayed that way.

As we pulled into their parking lot, well within time thanks to Dave's Grand Prix style driving abilities, he told me that once we got inside he wanted me to keep quiet and just observe. If he wanted me to say anything he'd ask me to. This didn't bother me a bit. I'd gladly let him run the meeting.

As we walked into the lobby Dave went to the reception window, and I wandered off to the side and looked around. I noticed a large glass display case showing the many products that T.C. manufactured. The walls were covered with what appeared to be ads for T.C. from industry magazines displayed in nice picture frames. Their brochures and a booklet about their company were neatly stacked on a table near the sofa. No doubt whose lobby we were in. It was a showplace for T.C. Healthcare.

The receptionist recognized Dave and greeted him like an old friend. He asked about her family. Dave was a pro, all right. When he wanted to he could be most charming. She let us go right in to the buyer's office.

The buyer was new to the company. Even though he and Dave had only met a few times before Dave made him feel like he was his best friend. He introduced me, and then they chatted for a few moments. Finally Dave got down to business.

"So Keith," Dave began, "Tony in our shipping department tells me that your receiving guys want their deliveries before 10 in the morning now. Tell me more about what you need."

"Dave, we've been growing way beyond our capacity. We have to make do with this building for now because we have a lease agreement, and because the plans for the new building are still being formed. We have to do twice as much work as we did only 18 months ago with the same facilities. With the quantity of orders we're sending out each day we don't have the space to accommodate trucks for deliveries and shipments at the same time.

"We need both docks after lunch available for trucks to pick up shipments. If we have one dock tied up because of a delivery, a pick-up driver might pass us up and come back later. Sometimes they get back late. Other times when they come back their trucks are so full the drivers don't have enough room to handle all we have to give them.

"Until we get a larger building, which won't be for at least a year and a half, we need to have all deliveries before noon so we can get our orders out in the afternoon. We don't have enough docks to ship and receive at the same time. We need your truck here as early as possible, preferably before noon. Can you do that for us?"

Dave wasn't expecting that explanation of why they needed earlier deliveries. He told me in the car on the way over that he suspected the problem was that the buyer wasn't placing his orders in time, and to make up for his delay he wanted everything delivered early in the morning. Dave told me it was becoming common for customers to pressure the sales reps to get early morning deliveries just for that reason.

While Dave sat there mulling over how to respond I spoke up and said, "Keith, what are we doing right for your company now?"

Dave looked at me in astonishment at first, then he narrowed his eyes and glared at me, silently telling me to keep my mouth shut as he'd told me to do.

"Bob, is it?" Keith said. "I've only been a buyer here for a few months, but it's obvious to me why my company buys from you guys. Everyone thinks highly of your company. We've never had a problem with quality as far as I know, and your drivers are very helpful and friendly. You're one of my best suppliers, by far. Believe me."

Dave's look softened a bit as he listened to Keith praise us.

Then I asked, "And Keith, what do we do that's wrong as far as you're concerned?"

Dave's eyes bulged as his grip crushed the arms of his chair. He kicked my leg under the desk and started to say something, but Keith cut him off.

"Like I said, you guys do a great job for us, but since you asked..."

Keith continued, "The one thing I have trouble with is getting a hold of Sheila, our rep. She does a great job for us, and I'm not ragging on her in any way, but it would help if she were able to respond quicker when I leave a message for her to call me."

After a short silence I asked, "Is there anything else that we're doing below your expectations?"

It was a good thing it was the 21st century. If Dave had had a sword in his belt I'm sure I'd have been beheaded by then. His face was redder than his tie.

"No, like I said, you guys really do an outstanding job."

"Keith," I said, "thanks for being so open with me. One last question, please. What else could we do to improve our service or products for you?"

I could see Dave start to calm down a little. He finally recognized that I was using the SWOT questions I'd told him about earlier. He was starting to understand what I was after.

Keith leaned back in his chair and gazed upward to think for a moment. Then he looked at Dave and me and said, "If Jensen can help us by getting deliveries in the morning, and Sheila had a faster way for us to get a hold of her that would be great. Everything else with your company is excellent."

Dave finally spoke and asked Keith if we could talk with the people in the warehouse to get a better idea of what exactly would work best for them. He also promised to find out how to help Sheila speed up her response time.

Keith took us back into the warehouse and introduced us to the shipping manager, Marty. Dave asked him about our deliveries.

Marty told us that at 2:00 p.m. each day a trucking company had an appointment to pick up shipments from T.C. He needed one dock cleared and available for them to pull in immediately or he risked the driver skipping him and coming back later with less room on the truck. Marty said he couldn't have any delivery trucks in the other dock then because other trucks came by sporadically in the afternoon to make pickups, too. As long as our truck was unloaded and out before 2:00 p.m., though, he said he'd have no problem with us making deliveries up until then. Marty told us that deliveries before 10:00 a.m. weren't necessary. He said that request came from someone who was over reacting to the situation.

With a better understanding of exactly what they needed, Dave told Marty he was confident he could commit to getting our trucks there before 2:00. He said he'd first need to check with our shipping department, but he promised to get back with him and Keith with a definite answer by the next day. He also gave Keith and Marty his business card with his cell-phone number handwritten on it and asked them to contact him if they had any problems whatsoever. Dave made it clear that he wasn't asking them to go around Sheila, but asked them not to hesitate and get him involved at their discretion.

Dave and I finally left with everyone smiling and talking about the new building and how great it'd be once it was completed.

As soon as we got in the car I started preparing for Dave to jump on me for opening my mouth. Instead he was quiet. The suspense of what he was thinking was making me nervous.

"Hey, I know you asked me to keep quiet, but I felt

the opportunity to ask those questions was too great to pass up," I finally said, breaking the silence.

"I gotta admit I was outraged at first," Dave said, "but when you got to the question about how could we improve, I found myself anxious to hear his answer. Like you were telling me in the car earlier, we need to find more customer wants to leverage our profit. Keith obviously wanted better communication from Sheila, and us.

"I was hoping to solve the delivery problem at this meeting, which I'm confident we will. But you uncovered another opportunity to do even more for them. I want to meet with Sheila and find out exactly what the problem is with returning Keith's calls. Once we solve it we'll stand an even better chance of out distancing the competition and expanding our business as they grow. If you hadn't asked the question we might never have known there was a problem.

"Also, while we were out in the warehouse I saw some possible applications for our products they aren't using now. Certainly they'll need them when they get into their new building. When I meet with Sheila I'm going to help her develop a plan to introduce those products to Keith before someone else does."

"You know," I said, "as we were driving over there I was thinking it was going to be a service call by taking care of a problem. But, if you saw an opportunity to sell them more products then I guess it was a sales call, too. There seems to be little distinction between sales and customer service."

"Interesting point," Dave said, as he pulled into our parking lot. "I hadn't thought of service as a part of sales, but, as you put it, perhaps we're in customer service as well as sales. Don't let the people in customer service hear that or they may want some of the commissions," he added with a smile.

He stopped his car near the front door to let me out. He told me he needed to leave right away to meet a customer for lunch. I asked him to try the SWOT questions with his customer and get back to me with the results. He sounded reluctant at first, but I got him to agree as he drove off.

Once I got inside the building I headed straight for Tony's office hoping to catch him before he left for lunch. I wanted to see if he could help with T.C. and get his driver there before 2:00 p.m. without disturbing deliveries to other customers. It turned out it wouldn't be too hard to make the adjustment. By doing so we had just added a T.C.'s 'want' to the left side of our plank, and hopefully moved the fulcrum a little to the right toward better service.

Afterwards I took a quick lunch in my office and made some notes about the meeting at T.C. Next on my agenda was a meeting with Walter Jensen. I was looking forward to it and didn't want to be late, so I brought up the list of questions I had for him on my computer and printed them. Then I headed down the hall to his office.

CHAPTER TWELVE

"Hi Nancy, is Walter ready for me yet?" I said as I walked into her office.

Nancy doubled as Walter and Allen's secretary. It was more a courtesy for Walter than a necessity. Luckily his work didn't impose on her much.

"He isn't back from lunch, yet, but go ahead and wait in his office. He should be in any minute now."

When I went into his office, I felt like I was walking into the past. The only modern item in the room was a computer tucked away in the corner of a credenza. The furniture was old, but well kept. The far wall looked like a family photo album. There was a picture of the first building the company occupied. Walter and his brother were standing beside an old Dodge parked in front of a brick building. As Mr. Jensen used to tell the story, that old car was his office, delivery truck and warehouse the first year he was in business.

Before I sat down Walter entered the room.

"Hello Bob, nice to see you. Have a seat," Walter

said as he walked slowly behind his desk and adjusted the blinds to let some light in.

"Hi Walter. How was your trip to headquarters?" I asked.

"It was fine," he said. "They sure use a lot of computers. It seems they have more information than they know what to do with. How can I be of help to you today?"

I filled him in on the marketing project. I told him how at first I tried to find where Neil had left off, but that there didn't seem to be a trail to follow. He just smiled and nodded as if he knew there wouldn't be anything to find.

I went on to tell him about my meetings with Uncle Phillip. I told him how I was discovering that marketing seemed to have less to do with sales and more with customers. I even shared with him what had happened that morning with Dave at T.C. and how I was beginning to see a connection between sales and customer service.

After I felt I'd explained my whole situation I asked him, "What was it like when you and Mr. Jensen started the company?"

He crossed his arms and leaned back, then stared at the wall of photos, smiling as if recalling fond memories.

"You know, when it was just James and me we did everything together except sell. That was his forte. He loved calling on customers. As soon as he'd have orders after calling on them all morning he'd rush back to the office and hand them over to me like a baton in a relay race. I'd outsource the materials while he'd be making calls to printers to schedule production. Then it was up to me to follow up on the orders until they were delivered so James could go out and get more orders. Once the orders shipped I'd invoice the customer and do collections to make sure we got paid.

"As the company grew, I gravitated toward the accounting end of the business, and James took over the hiring of people to help us. All the while he continued to call on customers. He still had three of his favorite accounts he'd held on to up until he died. He felt it kept his finger on the pulse of the business."

"So," I asked, "what kind of marketing did the two of you do when you started out?"

"Well, that's a good question. I don't know that we ever did any marketing per se. James would always say, 'take care of the customer' and he made sure that everything we did focused on that. If he couldn't see how a new idea or product or technology helped him serve a customer better he wasn't interested in it.

"He explained his philosophy to me one night when we were working late by ourselves. It was quite simple. 'Only do those things that serve a customer, and do them so well the customer will want to do business with us again.' He said the only way we ever got any business was through referrals and that there were two types.

"The first type was if a customer liked what he received, he'd tell other people about it and refer them to us. He said a customer would also refer himself back to us if we did a good enough job for him."

"Interesting way to look at it," I said. "A customer referring himself to do business with you again."

"But," Walter went on, "we always needed to follow up. If a customer was ever unhappy in any way we needed to know about it for two reasons.

"First, if we didn't know about it we'd never be able to fix it for that customer or for others in the future. And second, if the customer didn't tell us about the problem he was sure to tell someone. And that would be the second type of referral—a dissatisfied customer referring business away from us."

I began thinking back to Phillip's story about the restaurant where he had to wait so long for his check. As a result of his experience alone I would never go there. He certainly wasn't going back either. One mistake lost them more than one dissatisfied customer; it lost them a future customer, too—me.

"Mr. Jensen sure knew a lot about business and people," I said. "I can't think of any other company that I'd want to work for, except maybe one that I would own. And if that were the case I'd model it after this one in every way I could."

"I'll tell you a secret. James felt that the better he treated his employees the better they would treat his customers. Any decision he made had to mutually help employees and customers."

I interrupted with, "I remember him telling a group of us when we were late from lunch one day that we were ignoring the customers. He told us that he didn't pay our salaries, the customers did. He said he only handled the transaction. He felt it was our job to be there waiting to take care of the customers so that we could get paid by them. He didn't say it in a condescending manner. He said it matter-of-factly. We all felt a little ashamed when he left the room. I felt like I'd let Mr. Jensen down."

"I'm sure he saw it as letting the customer down,

not him," Walter said.

"So he made all his decisions based on the customer and workers, huh?" I was thinking out loud, more than saying it to Walter.

"When he made any decision about what products to sell it was always based on the customers' needs. Even when we moved to this building he chose this location because it was more central and easier to access than any others that he looked at. He was offered a site outside of town, but he thought the money he would save in taxes and land would be lost because of the inability of sales to really serve the customers."

"He sure did put an emphasis on the sales force," I said, remembering how pampered I felt when I was in sales.

"That's because he knew that a sales rep was the customer when he walked in the office. Actually the rep only represented a customer, but he treated that person like a king or queen as long as he or she was doing work for a customer.

"I don't want you to get the idea that James was so concerned about customers and employees that he wasn't concerned about money. He was just as concerned about making a profit, too. He just didn't let the customers or employees know it.

"It was my job to make sure our expenses were minimal. When we pinched pennies around here everyone always thought it was because of me. I was often seen as the bad guy, but it was always James driving me to keep costs down."

"That's interesting," I said, thinking back. "I always thought you were the frugal one and that Mr. Jensen fought to get the money from you for raises and such."

"That's how he wanted it to look. But don't think it was wrong. He believed that customers, employees and profits were all intertwined. He believed that you couldn't have one without the other two. He focused his attention on the customers and employees and left me to focus on the profits. Think about the different combinations possible between customers, employees and profits.

"You can have customers and no employees, as he did when he started in business, but the profits were limited. As one person he could only call on so many companies and do so much of the work himself.

"You could have customers and employees with no profit, but not for long. Eventually you'd go out of business. Everyone deserves a reward for his or her effort; otherwise, what's the point?

"And the third combination you'd have only employees and profit, but that's impossible. With no customers where would the profit come from, and what work would the employees have to do?

"The only successful combination needs all three present for everyone to win."

I thought about Phillip's formula—Customer Wants times Satisfaction minus Expenses equals Profit—and told Walter about it.

"That's very interesting" Walter said as he pondered the idea.

After some thought he said, "I can see where the minus for expenses comes from. But it would seem to me the multiplication of the customer's satisfaction comes from the employees. The employees take care of the customers. James took care of the employees. I made sure there were profits. It seems to fit your formula, doesn't it?"

"It does," I said. "So what you're saying is Mr. Jensen considered all of those in his decisions about the company?"

"Employees, customers and profit—what else makes up a business?" Walter asked.

It was a rhetorical question, of course. He wasn't expecting an answer.

Our meeting ended there. I felt like I knew Mr. Jensen better than I ever did when he was alive. I used to feel sorry for Walter because he had sold out his shares of the company and never got to benefit from the growth that he helped create. He didn't seem bothered by it, though. He was still proud to have been a part of the company. Maybe Mr. Jensen took care of him in a way no one else would ever know. Regardless, it was obvious that Walter was happy with his life as it was.

After I left his office and walked back to mine I realized I didn't have anything else scheduled that day. I had a lot to mull over. I felt like I needed a mental break—something completely different to get my mind off the project for a while.

It was early in the afternoon and I thought of slipping out. If I left I figured I could stop by the high school and catch Josh at football practice. Some fresh air and some family time—that would be a perfect way to end the day.

CHAPTER THIRTEEN

W hen I walked through the field's gate I saw the freshman team practicing and wondered how I'd be able to pick Josh out from all the other players. The practice jerseys were plain white and didn't have numbers on them. Some of the boys had colored vests to distinguish them from the starting players during a practice scrimmage. I figured Josh would be in that group. He wasn't a starter — yet.

While I was trying to detect Josh's face inside one of the helmets his good friend Kyle walked up to me.

"That's him playing right-guard on the offense, Mr. Hayden."

"I thought the first string wore the plain shirts," I asked. The player he pointed out didn't have a vest on.

"They do. Coach has Josh working with them."

"Josh is on the first team?" I asked, excited at the thought.

"No. Coach is rotating some of the guys in so they'll be more familiar with the plays in case they need to fill in for someone during a game."

I didn't expect Josh to be doing that well so soon. It was a good strategy on the coach's part. I remember when I played football the attitude was unless you were on the first team, why bother to learn the plays. The chance that anyone other than the first team would actually get to play was remote because the coach never used anyone but his best players in a game. Even in practice the rest of us were just tackling dummies for the starters. If you didn't stand out as a super player at the beginning of the year you sat on the bench for the rest of it.

As I watched Josh run some plays, someone else approached me from the side.

"Hello, I'm Coach Neilson. And you are?"

"I'm Bob Hayden, Josh's father," I said, startled to meet the coach. "Nice to meet you."

"Same here. Just wanted to make sure you weren't a spy from another team," he said as he held out his hand to shake mine.

This was the guy that Josh was so thrilled about, I thought? He didn't look like the macho, strict disciplinarian I'd pictured. He had a warm smile and an easy demeanor. He was tall, but didn't come across intimidating. I could see why Josh looked up to him as he did.

"Josh is a good kid," he said. "Not much experience, but a quick learner."

"That he is," I said, unable to think of much else to say.

Then he cupped his hands to his face and called to another coach to have the players run a lap and then do some stretching before they finished for the day. The coach turned toward me and asked if I'd seen any of their games yet.

"Every one. I want to support my son as much as I can," I said, hesitating to add that I hadn't seen him play in one yet.

"Josh has told me some very interesting stuff about your coaching philosophy. Your goal isn't to win, eh?"

With a bit of a chuckle he replied, "I hear a lot about that from parents."

"I'm not knocking it," I said, a bit embarrassed that he might have thought I was putting him down. "I think it's quite interesting. How'd you come across it?"

"I'm not sure if you know my background. I was the president of Bleuth Industries until I retired a couple of years ago. I've been an assistant coach with the varsity and junior varsity the last few years. When the position for the freshmen coach came up it was offered to me and I took it. I just use the same ideas to motivate and guide the players that I used with my employees."

I was thinking, 'He ran Bleuth? The largest company in the valley?' I began to recognize him from photos in the paper I'd seen from time to time.

"Teamwork in the workplace isn't much different than on the playing field," he said. "I want the boys to learn that it's a group effort that wins games, not individuals. Either we're all pulling together toward the same goal or our energy is scattered and not as efficient or effective.

"When I was in charge at Bleuth I believed every person in the company was there for a purpose. No one was extraneous. Some workers may have seemed more important than others only because of their visibility, but I wanted each person to know, no matter what his or her position was, that he or she was just as important as anyone else in the company.

"I used to tell them that the engine of a car weighs hundreds of pounds and makes a lot of noise compared to the small brake cylinder that sits next to it under the hood. A car would be in trouble, though, without that small cylinder. If the car didn't have an engine it couldn't go forward and wouldn't need the brakes. If the brakes weren't in place the car's motion caused by the engine would create a danger. The engine was larger and made more noise than the brake cylinder, but both were dependent on each other to reach any goal safely.

"The same is true with these players—each one contributes to the whole. Together they make up a team. Some are bigger; some are smaller. Some work hard when playing against another team, and others work just as hard here at practice. I tell them that if they're on my team they're just as important as anyone else."

"Makes sense," I said. "Well, you're certainly doing a fine job. Two wins no losses. I look forward to seeing your next game."

The coach glanced at the boys who were about to finish their stretching and excused himself. He jogged over to them and gathered them around for some parting words to end the practice.

I waited outside the gym for Josh so I could give him a ride home. Once he saw me standing there he appeared to lower his head a bit. He didn't look pleased about something.

"Hey Josh, you don't mind that I stopped by to see

you practice do you?"

"Well, no Dad. Where's Mom? I thought she was picking me up today. She usually just waits in her car in the parking lot."

"I called her and told her I'd pick you up today. Everything okay?"

I couldn't imagine why the long face, and then it dawned on me.

"Are you embarrassed because I showed up at your practice?" I asked.

"Well, it just looks funny, you talking with the coach, you know? Nobody said anything, but I felt like they were thinking that you were acting like Billy's dad trying to get in good with the coach so he'd play me more."

"I'm sorry son. That never even occurred to me. I didn't plan on talking with the coach. He came up to me. You understand don't you?"

Josh said he did. He knew I wouldn't do anything like that.

"How about we stop for a soda and some fries on the way home?" I suggested.

He looked up at me with the start of a smile and said, "Sure!"

So we got in the car and drove off. On our way Josh began to tell me about the plays he was learning. The excitement in his voice told me he was over any embarrassment.

"So, still like your coach?" I said.

"Who wouldn't?" he said. "He's tough, but fair. I don't think there's a guy on the team who hasn't gotten to play with the first team yet; at least at practice."

"You looked pretty good out there. Think you'll get

to play this week?"

"There's nothing I'd rather do, but you know, I'm happy just being a part of the team. Coach treats us all the same, like everyone's a starter."

"Are you still focused on your goal of four yards per down?" I asked.

"Actually Coach has refined it even further. He told the guys on the line and me that all we need to do is block our opponent for three seconds on running plays and five on pass plays. We don't have to knock them to the ground or keep them blocked forever, just long enough for the ball carrier to get past the line."

"That sounds pretty easy," I said.

"It's not that easy, but I have no doubt what I'm supposed to do to help the team succeed. Each position has its own assignment, too. All we need to do is our part and trust the other players to do theirs. As long as we do our best Coach said he'll respect us regardless of the outcome of the game."

"You obviously know your place on the team and how you contribute. Do you think the other players feel the same?" I asked.

"Coach wouldn't have them on the team if they didn't. I think that's why I'm enjoying it so much. I know how I fit in. I know what my task is. If the team succeeds I know exactly how the effort I produced contributed to the outcome of the game."

Produce I thought. That was a familiar word. "A customer is anyone who receives what we produce." If each worker knew exactly how his job contributed to the overall success of the company, would he have a better chance of enjoying what he did, just like Josh?

I wondered.

"Dad, are you listening?" Josh said.

My attention snapped back to Josh.

"Of course. I'm so glad you enjoy being a part of the team, and that you're able to see how you contribute, too. It feels good to be needed, doesn't it?"

Josh nodded and then reached to turn up the radio to hear a song he said was his favorite.

As he got caught up in the music I began to wonder again what would happen if everyone at the company understood exactly how he or she contributed to the company's success. Better yet, how he or she contributed to the company's purpose, and how every job ultimately serves a customer.

It made me feel good to finally see Josh play football, even if it was only at practice. I still hoped I'd get to see him play in a real game soon. At least he was having fun. What more could I ask?

CHAPTER FOURTEEN

I sat in my office staring at a pile of notes. I was trying to decide which ones to share with the managers later that afternoon. While I reached for my coffee to take a quick break and glance out the window, I noticed Naomi's report on my credenza that she'd dropped off the day before.

After Dave and I had our meeting with T.C. Healthcare I asked Naomi if she had heard any complaints about Sheila not returning the buyer's phone calls. She said no and asked if I'd heard of any.

I told her about the call Dave and I made to T.C. to resolve the early delivery situation. I also shared with her the three SWOT questions I'd asked the buyer — what we did right, what we did wrong and how could we improve. She said she could answer those questions for a lot of companies if they ever asked her. Actually, it wasn't always necessary to ask for Naomi's opinion in order to get it. She usually told people what she was thinking even when they didn't want to know.

She asked what I thought of her using the questions with her internal customers, the ones she'd listed in the exercise at last week's production meeting. I thought it was a great idea, and asked her to get back to me with what she found. That was the report on my credenza.

I grabbed her notes and started to read them. She'd discovered quite a bit. I decided to add her information with some of the other items I was going to present at the manager's meeting. Maybe the managers could do the same thing in their departments. The big coup would be to get Hankins to have his sales reps use the SWOT questions with customers. External customer feedback would help develop the marketing plan. I even considered going to the next sales meeting and asking the reps the questions. I pictured it turning into one big bitch session if it wasn't handled right, though. I wasn't sure if I wanted to go through with it or not. In the meantime, it would be worth presenting it that afternoon to management.

While I was reorganizing my presentation for the sixth time Carla popped her head through the door as she knocked.

"Hey, got a minute?" she asked.

"Sure. Come in."

"I need your help with some problems I'm having with one of our suppliers. Did you have many errors with Watson Brothers when you were buying from them?"

"Maybe one or two in several years, and those weren't much to mention. I don't remember exactly what they were. What's up?"

"I've had three orders in the last few weeks come in with the wrong material. Thank goodness they were always able to exchange them, but I'm worried that one of these times it'll be for a custom item and they won't take it back, or we won't have enough time to exchange it for the right material without delaying a customer's order."

"Do you know what the cause is?"

"I'm not sure. I hope it's not me, because I'm new to the account. I was requesting the same items from previous orders, but somehow they ended up wrong."

"Have they asked you to do anything different from before?"

"No. I thought I was doing it like you used to."

I stopped and thought about it for a moment. Something must have been different, something so minor that it appeared the same, but different enough to cause a problem. Then an idea came to me.

"Carla, if we use our definition of a customer as someone who receives what we produce, let's look at this as if Watson's our customer."

"But we're the customer. They should be helping us," she said with exasperation.

"Yes, I know. But for some reason that's not what's happening. Since we're the ones burdened when there's a problem, regardless of who's to blame, let's see if we can solve it for them. We'd really be solving it for ourselves, don't you think?"

"I guess so."

"Why don't you try this? Get the sales rep from Watson on the phone and ask him these questions. Perwin still handles our account, right?"

"Yeah."

"Here, I want you to write these down."

I handed her a yellow pad of paper as she took out a pen.

"First, ask him what we do now that he likes about our order process.

"Next, ask him what he doesn't like about how we do business with Watson. Don't settle for a superficial answer such as 'All's well.' Push him to find out what our weaknesses are when we place orders with him.

"Finally, ask Perwin what we could do to improve the way we place our orders so that it's easier for him to process them and to eliminate possible mistakes on either of our parts. Do you have all that?"

"Yes. I'll do it, but he's going to think I'm crazy."

"Please, do it for me, and let me know what happens."

I asked her how everything else was going and offered to help her if she had any extra work. I wished she'd say she had something I could've helped with. I wanted to do something other than meetings and reports for a change. But she said everything else was fine.

I looked at the clock and saw that I'd better get going. I had an appointment with the dentist. I was in no hurry to go there. More accurately, I just wanted to get it over with as soon as possible.

Sitting in the dentist's lobby made me uncomfortable; and I was only in for a check-up. I don't know why I was so nervous about being there. I guess all the cavities I had as a kid left some lingering memories.

The receptionist finally led me to the usual room. I looked around. There was the same ear-piercing drill and the same minty odor in the air. I settled into the chair and continued reading an old magazine I'd brought in from the lobby.

When the hygienist walked through the door, though, I looked up and noticed some new plaques on the wall. She started cleaning my teeth right away, so I didn't get a chance to talk with her much. But I kept reading what was written on the plaques and thinking about what they said.

Finally she was done.

Several minutes later the dentist walked in for the fun, probing part of the visit.

"Good day Mr. Hayden. How have your teeth been lately?"

"Fine," I said, getting more nervous with each shiny, sharp instrument he laid on the tray in front of me. He was always so stoic and unemotional, sort of robotic. That didn't help my nerves, either.

"I see you have some new plaques on your wall," I said, trying to keep my focus off of the instruments.

"Just trying to get a point across to my patients. Glad you noticed."

"I was reading them and thinking how they pertained to my work."

"Really?" he asked. "How's that?"

"Well, that one reads, 'You don't have to floss all your teeth—just the ones you want to keep.' That reminds me of our business. We don't have to take care of all our customers, just the ones we want to keep."

"Don't you want to keep all of them?" he asked.

He's a good dentist, but not much of a businessperson.

"Of course we do. That's the point. Sometimes workers forget how they need to treat customers. The whole purpose of their job is to serve them. If they don't serve them someone else will, and we don't want that. We need to take care of all our customers."

"Oh, I get it now," he said with as much emotion as his latex gloves.

"And that other one that says, 'Ignore your teeth and they'll eventually go away.' That reminds me of customers, too. A customer should never be ignored, even for a second."

"Boy, I should carry that sign around with me when I go to some restaurants. Talk about being ignored," he said with a bit of an edge to his voice. "I can't stand having to wait a long time for my check after I've finished my meal."

After probing around a little he said, "Well Mr. Hayden it looks like you haven't been ignoring your teeth. They look excellent. I won't get to poke you very much today after all."

He sounded disappointed, but he must have been joking. At least it was over quickly. But he reminded me that on my next visit he'd have to update my X-rays.

Before I left his office I jotted down the words from the plaques. I wanted to share them at work. I thought of printing them and handing them out at the manager's meeting that afternoon, if I had enough time.

Unlike Tuesday morning production meetings, the one that afternoon was for managers only. I'd only started attending the biweekly meetings about two years before Mr. Jensen died. It was enough time, though, to see the difference between the meetings then and what they had evolved to.

These days we'd discuss the same re-occurring topics

—how to increase productivity, company morale, the budget and other non-important things like the lack of parking and the company picnic. What seemed different, other than the absence of Mr. Jensen and his sons, was that fewer changes took place after the meetings. I sensed that the meetings lacked direction. Everyone wanted to think everything over before making a commitment. A lot of times it seemed items were forgotten rather quickly.

Since there were never more than 10 of us at a meeting we met in the small conference room adjacent to Allen's office. It was Carla's first meeting since she'd taken over my job as purchasing manager. She was the first one there. No doubt she wanted to make a good first impression.

The odd thing about those meetings was you didn't want to show up too early because it looked like you were wasting time. And you certainly didn't want to be late and interrupt it. The trick was to get there in just enough time to sit down, say hi to everyone, get out your papers and begin.

Dave knew the tacit attendance rule and followed right behind me, with Rudy, Naomi, and Tony trailing him. Then Allen opened his office door to let Nancy enter, and he appeared after her. Nancy was always present to keep the minutes.

After everyone was seated, Walter Jensen walked in and sat down. He hadn't been to a meeting in months. He'd been spending much of his time at the corporate offices. I was glad to see him. His presence added an air of importance to whatever we did.

Allen started at the top of the agenda with Dave's

sales report and went down the list calling each manager in turn to give his or her report.

I waited nervously until it was my turn. I wasn't quite sure exactly what I was going to say and was concerned about what kind of reaction I'd get.

Allen turned to me and said, "Now we'll hear from Bob."

I took one last look at my notes, cleared my throat and dove right in.

"I need your help," I began. "You're aware of my project—a plan to expand our market and profits.

"Last time I shared with you the idea that we're in the business of serving customers and that money is only a result of that purpose, not the goal in itself. Only after we serve a customer and deduct expenses do we have a chance of earning any profit."

I walked to the whiteboard and wrote Phillip's formula on it: $(CW \times S) - E = P$. I explained what each letter stood for—CW for customer wants, S for satisfaction, E for expenses, and P for profit. Then, instead of giving an explanation, I asked them what they thought about it.

After discussing it, they came to the same conclusion I had—that the process begins with the customer.

Then I drew the plank on the fulcrum and described its components. Again I asked their opinion, and again they reached the logical conclusions. Rudy pointed out what I had noticed when Phillip showed the drawing to me.

"The position of the fulcrum," Rudy said, "can make quite an impact on how much effort is needed to raise the lever. If the fulcrum is to the far left it would take an incredible amount of customer wants to raise the right side. Theoretically, if the fulcrum were at the very left edge, no amount of wants would be enough to raise the plank; in fact, everything would be on the right side holding down profits."

Then he asked, "What determines where the fulcrum is positioned? Wouldn't it be an advantage to have it near the right of the plank where fewer customers wants would be needed to raise the right side of the plank? Also, what keeps the fulcrum from drifting to the left where more customer wants would be needed to raise the plank and raise profits?"

I saw several managers nod in agreement with what Rudy had pointed out. If there was a way to keep the fulcrum near the center, what was it?

I was determined not to give them the answer, so I turned the question over to the group to see what they would say.

Carla was the first to raise her hand.

"Well, I'm just thinking about my own experience as a customer. It seems to me that the grocery store I shop at has hundreds of things I want, which makes it convenient for me. The large number of items they supply weighs a lot and raises the right side of their so-called plank. Even with the fulcrum to the left, they do okay because they have so many items to offer. They don't offer much in the way of service, but I guess they don't have to if they can meet so many wants. But I'm also thinking about a place I shop at that only meets one of my wants.

"My youngest daughter takes art lessons. When she finishes a painting I need to buy a frame for it. I found an art store that I've gone to several times. They only meet one want, that of having a frame, but the way they do it keeps me coming back.

"I first went to them because another frame shop I used to go to didn't have a frame for one of the paintings. The service at that store was okay, not bad, but it wasn't great, either.

"One day they didn't have any frames that went with my daughter's newest picture. They suggested I come back in a week or so to see if they had any new frames by then. I thought their attitude was somewhat indifferent about serving me, especially a repeat customer. I didn't want to wait a week or more. I wanted a frame that day. So I drove over to a new shop that had just opened.

"I went inside and right away found a frame I liked. I went to the counter to pay for it, and they put the picture in the frame for me, just like the other store. But when they handed it back to me they did something extra that the other shop had never done. They handed me a little bag with a hanger and nail inside to attach to the wall so I could hang the picture up as soon as I got home. And it was free.

"I was so pleased that I never went back to the old frame shop. Every time I visit the new one they make it such a pleasant experience by helping me pick out the right frame, and they always remember to include the free hanger.

"I've gone there ever since, adding to their profit. Since they only need to meet a single want, because I only have one for them to fulfill, I'd say that the level of service they've given me is what keeps their fulcrum near the center and allows them to profit from it.

She summed it up and said, "The grocery store raises profit by meeting a large number of wants, whereas the frame shop raises profit by increasing service. Does that make sense?"

On the whiteboard I drew an arrow under the fulcrum pointing left and right. To the left of the arrow I wrote "Less Service" and to the right I wrote "Greater Service."

"You're absolutely right, Carla," I said.

Turning to the entire group I explained, "So you can see, there are two ways to increase profits—to add more wants or to increase the level of service."

Rudy said, "It would seem that the quickest way to increase profits would be to add wants and increase the level of service at the same time."

"Sounds like," Dave spoke out, "Ben Franklin's advice to get rich. He said we should either diminish our wants or augment our means. The quickest way, he said, was to do both at the same time. The same is true here. Add wants or increase service. The best way would be to do both at the same time."

"So how do we do both, Bob?" Allen asked, as if on cue.

"I'm glad you asked. If you accept the theory of the lever and fulcrum it leads us to what we need to focus on in the formula. We can increase profits by reducing our expenses, but they can only be reduced so much. The two places where we can have the greatest impact and increase profits is by focusing on improving the level of service our customers receive and by satisfying more customer wants. The quickest way, as Dave pointed out, is to do both.

"Since the formula begins with the customer, I believe the most efficient way to go about this is to start with our customers and ask them what they expect and want from us. We need to hear it directly from them; otherwise, if we try and guess what they want we may be wrong. Here's how we can be sure we know what their wants and expectations are . . . ."

I shared the three SWOT questions with them by writing them on the whiteboard. Dave supported me by telling them about our visit to T.C. Healthcare. He employed his usual dramatics to add flare to the story and made it sound like we saved the company from losing thousands of dollars by keeping one of the company's biggest accounts. Of course Dave exaggerated, but it helped get the point across.

I also shared Naomi's experience with them about what she'd discovered by asking one of her internal customers, our purchasing department, those questions.

She'd found out that when a customer was ordering a custom item for the first time, one of our customer service people had to get all the pertinent information for the new job and put it onto an order form. Then the form was sent to purchasing to buy the needed materials. When purchasing got the form, though, they needed to transcribe much of the information to a job folder. That folder then traveled throughout the company as the order was processed from purchasing to production to the warehouse and finally to shipping. The folder then was placed in a permanent file.

Because of what Naomi had discovered, some changes were made. The blank job folders are now in the customer service department instead of purchasing. The customer service people write the information directly on the job folder as they take the information from the customer. The form was revised. Redundant information was removed, questions were shortened and the type was enlarged for better readability.

When production needs to use the form later in the process only the information they need is on it, nothing extra.

The result was that customer service people didn't have to write so small. Purchasing didn't have to transcribe anything at all. And in the end, production still got all the information they needed only much more legibly. Everyone was pleased. All because someone asked, "What can we do to improve what we do for you?"

I also explained how important our last impression with a customer is and how their perception about us could change over time and so could our service, so it would be necessary to survey our customers regularly.

I then handed out sheets with one of the sayings I copied from the dentist's office — *You don't need to floss all your teeth, just the ones you want to keep.*

I said that the same was true of our customers. The ones we wanted to keep needed to be asked the three SWOT questions. At the bottom of the sheet were the other plaque's words — *Ignore your teeth and they'll go away.*

When all the questions ended I thanked everyone, walked back to my chair and sat down.

Allen walked to the front of the room staring at the questions I'd written on the whiteboard.

"Bob, have any other departments done this yet?"

he asked.

"They've each identified their internal customers, but only Naomi has used the questions so far," I said.

"I want to know the internal customers of each department. I want every manager to find the answer to these questions." Then he looked at Dave and said, "And what about your reps? How soon can they start using them with customers?"

Before Dave could answer I spoke up and said, "I'm going to make this presentation to the sales group at their next meeting. Then they'll be able to use it with customers."

"Our next meeting is this Monday," Dave added, as if he'd already planned the meeting with me.

"Good," Allen said.

Right then, Walter stood up from his seat at the back of the conference table. Everyone turned his way.

"Allen, may I?" he asked.

Allen nodded and sat down.

"When James and I were the only ones here we didn't have departments. We handled everything by ourselves.

"I was responsible for several jobs and he took responsibility for the rest. As we grew we had to hire people to help us. They took over some of our responsibilities. As the number of employees increased some had to specialize at a job. As we continued to expand and had more than one person doing a similar job it became a department. Now the company has several. That's a natural occurrence for any growing company.

"What has always stayed the same, though, as Bob has pointed out, is what James and I did in the beginning—help each other do our jobs. This idea of serving each other is what we've always done.

"If we now consider each other as 'customers' that seems reasonable. And if that's true, then aren't we all in customer service?"

It was silent for a moment before Carla said: "It appears that way."

The rest of the group nodded in agreement.

"And," Walter went on, "if each of us has an impact on external customers, indirectly if not directly, then why are only some of our employees considered to be in customer service? Isn't every department customer service? Shouldn't they be called the operator/customer service department? The order entry/customer service department? The purchasing/customer service department? And all departments slash customer service?"

I raised my hand and asked, "Walter, I think you're right, but wouldn't it be more appropriate for the department to start with the words customer service first and then what they do to serve a customer, such as customer service/shipping department?"

"That sounds even better, Bob," Walter said as he gave me a smile. "The whole idea sounds trivial, I imagine, but it sure would demonstrate to everyone where we expect the emphasis to be — on the customer."

"It seems the more I delve into marketing, the more it has to do with the customer," I said.

"That's what James was always telling us — take care of the customer. If we're going to meet Consolidated's expectations we can't do it alone. We're going to need the help of our customers."

Then Walter sat down. He said what he had to say.

Allen looked at his watch and concluded the meeting. It was after 6:00 p.m. Everyone wanted to get back to his or her office and wrap up the day and head home.

Allen turned to Nancy and told her what to write for the summary that would go out to each of us the next morning. I imagined what I'd be doing. I had a feeling the three SWOT questions were going to multiply my project, but I was glad. I was beginning to see precisely what the marketing plan was going to become. I looked forward to finally putting it together and realized the next step was to get the sales department to help me.

CHAPTER FIFTEEN

Sales meeting night was when Dave Hankins shined. He loved being in front of his troops. He thrived on going over the previous month's numbers and singling out the record-breaking high achievers. Dave was like a big brother to the reps who looked to him for guidance, encouragement and a boost in confidence. He was the ideal sales manager. He wasn't just great at selling but at managing and motivating people, too. He knew to praise individuals in front of their peers but to reprimand in private. He was tough, but always fair. I was glad he was on our team and not a competitor's.

Not everyone liked him, though. Those who didn't left the company. Some thought he was just too hard on people. But Dave was also hard on himself; he just expected the same dedication from others.

If you did your job well the numbers would show it, and Dave would be your friend. If you did your job exceptionally well the numbers would show it, and

Dave was your best buddy and would yell from the rooftops what an outstanding salesperson you were. But, if you did your job poorly the numbers would show that, too, and then you wouldn't even want to know Dave.

Dave didn't believe in meeting people half way. He'd give you one hundred percent every time, and he expected you to do the same. He'd help you in every way he could, but if you didn't at least help yourself you'd get nothing from him. If you were honest with yourself you always knew where you stood with Dave.

The meeting that night was his favorite kind. A sales contest had just ended and he had the privilege of handing out the awards. Top prize that night was a dinner for two at any nice restaurant in town, with limo transportation. Dave didn't want his top salesperson celebrating too much then having to drive anywhere. He wanted him or her safely back on the street and making calls the next day.

The chairs in the lunchroom had been rearranged and the tables pushed to the side for the meeting. It was the only room large enough to hold 14 salespeople and the several managers and guests that were usually there. I was a guest that night.

When the meeting started I sat in the back of the room. Dave was up front, behind the lectern. He was glowing with enthusiasm over the numbers he displayed on an overhead projector. As he announced each victory the group roared with applause and cheers.

When all but the last category had been announced Dave paused to build the tension. He stroked the paper in his hands that held the numbers of the top salesperson for the quarter. He read each number as if the impossible had been obtained. He displayed nothing less than astonishment with every word he spoke. Although Dave didn't let on, everyone knew who the winner was going to be—again. Yet the applause still came loudly when he announced Jeff's name and asked him to step forward to accept the award.

After all the hoopla was over the meeting became less formal. People were chatting about how business was and the big orders they almost had. But Dave cut it short and told everyone that I was there for a special presentation. He said that if they wanted to make more sales they'd better listen closely to what I had to say. I walked to the front of the room hoping I'd live up to his expectations.

After I said hello to the group, I asked, "Why do people buy from Jensen Printing?"

"Service," someone said.

"Be more specific," I replied. "What does service mean to your customers?"

"A quality product."

"On time delivery."

"Knowledgeable salespeople."

"Quick response time."

Several other people called out more answers at random.

"Can't they get those from your competitors?" I challenged them. I knew those were the same reasons we gave all the time from my years in sales. They were also the same claims our competition made.

"They don't get me," Jeff volunteered.

"And what makes you different from your

competitors, Jeff?" I asked.

"None of them work as hard as I do or care as much about them as I do," he said with a grin of confidence.

"That's the difference. How much you care about your customers. You care that they get on-time deliveries. You care that they get a quality product. They buy from you because you care enough to be interested in helping them, isn't that right?"

Jeff, and everyone, nodded in agreement.

"That's what service is. Service is interest—your genuine interest in your customer," I said. Then I paused to let them absorb that idea.

I put an overhead on the projector that read, "Our purpose is to serve customers." Below the statement was the fulcrum and lever drawing from Uncle Phillip.

I spent the next several minutes walking them through the theory of Phillip's formula.

"So, if the two variables that we have control over are the number of wants we supply and the level of satisfaction the customer receives, how can we expand our business?"

"We need to find out what they want and what it takes to satisfy them," answered Gloria, a newer sales rep with the company.

"Bob, that's great," Jose said condescendingly. "That's the most basic part of selling. When you call on a new prospect any half-decent salesperson knows to qualify him with a needs-analysis questionnaire. If you find he has no need for what you do you go on to the next prospect and do the same thing until you find someone who does qualify. You were in sales, you already know this stuff."

"Yes I do," I replied, "and few are better at it than you Jose. You've opened more new accounts than anyone here," I said, hoping a little flattery would keep him quiet for a while.

Then Dave stood up to take some of the pressure off of me and said, "Jose, what Bob is getting at is the fact that once we open an account we seldom go back and qualify them again. When was the last time you sat down with a buyer and asked them specifically how we're doing?"

Jeff sat there a moment and then said, "I always ask him if there is anything I can do to help him on every call."

"And when I make calls on your behalf as the manager I ask the same thing, 'How are we doing?' and I always hear the same response you probably get, 'You're doing fine, you're already helping me.'

"We need to find out more than that. We're in sales—we sell. What Bob is talking about is marketing. If we want to get more sales and increase our commissions we also need to become marketers to our accounts. That's what he's getting at. This may sound simple, but let's at least hear him out." Then he turned to me and said, "Bob, go on."

"You guys know what to do, you're the top producers in our industry. I'm not asking you to do anything different. What I want you to be aware of are three questions that will give you more information and could allow you to be of greater help to your customers than you are today."

I then put the questions on the overhead and went over each one in detail. I emphasized their importance to answering what our strengths, weaknesses, opportunities and threats were. I even used the story of the restaurant experience that Phillip related to impress upon them the need to use those types of questions and not just asking if everything was okay.

I told them about my son's football coach and his unusual attitude of not focusing on winning but on all the little things that you do so that winning is the end result. I told them that we needed to do the same. Although, we couldn't ignore the fact that we needed a larger return for Consolidated, I wanted them to understand that if we'd focus on satisfying more customer wants the result should be the increase in sales we needed.

Dave pointed out that it went along with our philosophy of relationship selling. The greatest service we could provide our customers, he said, was to find more and better ways to serve them. Then he sat down and let me continue.

"You're the closest contact the company has to customers. You work with them more than anyone else in the company. For the most part you are the customer when you walk in the office or call here on the phone. You represent the customer to the rest of us.

"Getting back to the questions, what else is a strength that we have that keeps our customers from going to our competition?"

I wrote down all the answers they gave me on the whiteboard. They were the usual ones: quick communication, speed, people that care and other obvious strengths.

"Now, what are our weaknesses?" I asked. So it didn't turn into a finger-pointing and whining session

I added, "We need to critique ourselves, not criticize each other, please."

I wrote down their answers on the whiteboard. Some items were expected, like our company being small, the long lead-time for custom orders and late deliveries. Possible problems with our accessibility came up. Interesting . . . I'd always thought we were very accessible to customers. Then I remembered Keith at T.C. Healthcare and his complaint of how hard it was for him to get a hold of his sales rep. It was obvious we needed to question everything we did for customers and not assume anything about our service.

"Now, what opportunities are in front of you right now that you've been overlooking? This is where you need to be creative, so don't hold back. What can you do in addition to what you're already doing?"

After a minute, Doug, a veteran sales rep, raised his hand. I nodded for him to speak.

"This is more like a threat we have, but maybe it's an opportunity, too. Many customers now have PCs with programs and printers that allow them to create their own forms. Some of my customers have replaced forms they used to buy from me. It was never a big threat because they were usually for single-sheet or two-part forms that were really a very small part of the dollars they spent with me. But still, it's been a loss.

"The opportunity part of this could be that since our customers do some of their own printing they use more plain paper. We've never solicited that business before. We buy large quantities of paper. I wonder if we could be competitive enough to supply our customers with plain paper? I'd bet that some of my accounts would buy it just for the convenience. I don't know. It's just a thought."

Gloria said, "I see a lot of my customers use the boxes our forms come in to store old files they have. They aren't really made for that. They're not as strong as regular record storage boxes. What if we offered a few of the stronger ones with each order, maybe at no-charge, as something a little extra?"

"Maybe we could even have our name printed on them. That way they would think of us when they need more storage boxes," another rep called out.

"I don't want to be a box salesman," said Jose. "I sell forms, custom forms. That's who I am." Jose didn't sound comfortable with the ideas that were coming out of the discussion.

"If that's how we see ourselves that's how the customers probably see us, too—just a supplier of forms," I said. "If we're going to expand our market we need to expand our own definition of what we do. Customers don't buy forms from us just to store on their shelves. What do they use our forms for?"

Jeff replied, "To organize information so it's easier to understand."

"Jensen Printing is more than forms, at least that's the message we need to get to our customers. We help them organize information. Record storage boxes, plain paper for their PCs, those also help them organize information."

"Maybe we can even help them with standard forms, or simple software to create their own forms with plain paper," Doug suggested.

"How are we going to compete on software

programs? Are we going to start developing software now?" Jose asked.

"Probably not, but we can do some research and find the best programs out there and then distribute them," Dave said. "That wouldn't be the main type of business we'd go after, just a convenience for those customers who would use it. That certainly won't be everyone. But everyone would see us as more than just printers. I like the idea.

"But you know," he continued, "I don't know that any of these ideas we've come up with are ever going to happen. I'm not saying they're bad ideas, either. But I do believe those questions need to be asked. We're only speculating about what our customers want. I think we need to take these ideas to them and see what they think. I also think that by asking our customers we may find other opportunities that we could never come up with on our own.

"Let's take these marketing questions to them and see what happens. If anything, our customers will see that we're trying to be of greater service and at least demonstrate how much we care and respect their ideas and input. I can't see any harm in trying this approach, and it can only be a positive experience, even if we come up with nothing more than to keep doing what we do now."

Dave took over from here. He asked the sales reps to begin using the questions with their customers immediately. He added that management would come up with other ways to solicit ideas from them, such as focus groups, or possibly using a third party to conduct surveys. Jose even agreed that if it were going to help his customers spend more money, then he'd support it in any way he could.

As soon as I gathered my notes and overheads Dave told me I could skip the rest of the meeting if I liked.

I decided to stay. I wanted them to see that I was more than just a manager dumping a project at their feet and walking away. I wanted to stick around and answer any questions about the formula or the lever and fulcrum theory.

I ended up being one of the last ones to leave that night. They did have a lot of comments to share with me about what we'd talked about. I needed their support more than the others at the company because of their close relationship with customers. After the meeting I was confident I had it, and management's support, too.

Next step was to gain the support of the people inside the company. I hoped it would go as well as it had with the sales team.

16

The plan was taking form. Seven weeks as the marketing manager and it finally felt like I was on track.

The sales force became comfortable using the SWOT questions and was uncovering opportunities for the company. Sales of new products and new applications for old products were trickling in. The key appeared to be promoting our strengths to customers. Not the strengths we thought we had, but the ones our customers told us they'd experienced.

The focus on weaknesses was having results, too. Any problems the reps uncovered were turned over to Dave who personally followed up on every complaint. He would assign someone to identify the cause and make any changes necessary. But, Dave would then follow up with the customer to make sure the problem was solved to his or her satisfaction when possible, not just to our satisfaction.

Dave called our new approach "Selling Through

Service." Once customers perceived us as being solution-oriented they viewed our reps as consultants instead of just salespeople.

When Dave looked into Keith's complaint from T.C. about the sales rep, Sheila, not returning calls fast enough he found out something interesting. Sheila was returning calls immediately, usually within fifteen minutes. Once Dave examined the situation more closely he found the problem wasn't with Sheila, but Keith's reluctance to use voicemail.

Here's what was happening. Keith would call our office and leave a message for Sheila to call him back but not give any other information to our operator. Sheila would call right back but Keith was seldom available and she ended up with his voicemail; having the operator page him rarely helped. All she could do then was leave him a message that she'd returned his call. But she couldn't leave him any information because she didn't know why he was calling. Even when Keith tried to call her cell phone he seldom got her if she was busy with another customer. They would play phone-tag for several hours before talking with each other.

Dave took the approach of identifying every means possible for the two of them to communicate. He gave Keith a direct number to Sheila's voicemail and set it up so that as soon as a message was recorded it paged her. Keith said he would state his request so that as soon as Sheila received the message she could act on it rather than waste time calling back several times just to find out what she needed to do.

Sheila committed to confirming with Keith

whatever action she was taking by leaving a response to his request on his machine when she was unable to reach him in person. That way Keith knew that she was at least working on it and would get back to him when she had an answer or to update him with whatever progress she had made if it was going to take a while. If they would leave messages with each other with specific information then direct conversation wouldn't always be necessary and problems could still be resolved.

Dave got Keith to give him all the possible ways for Sheila to get in touch with him, including his personal cell phone number. Dave emphasized that the cell phone was to be used only if Keith's request was an emergency; otherwise, Sheila would use voicemail.

Dave followed up with Keith a month later to see if things had improved. Keith had no complaints. In fact, he appreciated the time he was saving by using voice-mail with Sheila. Regarding emergency calls, only once did he have one, and Sheila was able to get a hold of him right away.

Dave had taken the original communication problem and turned it into an opportunity. Keith now had a more convenient way to communicate with Sheila better than any other competitor because Dave pursued the question "How can she reach you better?" Not that any other supplier couldn't have done the same thing, but we had an edge simply because we asked. Unfortunately, Sheila had tried a similar approach herself, but it really worked when the request came from Dave as a manager.

Sheila was pleased with the outcome. It was less

frustrating for her to deal with Keith by eliminating unproductive calls. If it took Dave to make it work that was okay with her.

Other changes had taken place, too, besides those with customers and sales.

I was in the meeting room and chatting with Naomi waiting for people to attend another production meeting. Carla walked in and thanked Naomi for the doughnuts. I wondered what that was all about?

"What were the doughnuts for?" I asked.

"Just a thank you to one of our customers. Carla's group completed the survey," she said.

"Survey?" I asked.

"The one created to monitor how well we're serving her department. Purchasing is one of our internal customers, and we thought we'd thank them with some doughnuts. Is that all right, Bob?"

"Well, sure, why not?" I stammered.

I'd noticed that people in the company were starting to treat each other differently. It began when we looked upon each other as customers. I must say it was a pleasant change. People were working to help each other. The competitive edge was gone.

When the meeting began, and it was my turn to speak I asked, "Remember the lists you gave me about who receives your output? Well, for the last week or so Rudy and I've used them to map the flow of work through the company. We found some interesting patterns. What we discovered was the relationship between external customers and certain departments, and the relationship among various departments in the company."

I put up an overhead that showed several circles, like a bulls-eye. The word "Customer" was in the center. In the outer circles were the names of all our departments.

"Looks like a map of the solar system, Bob," Gene called out.

"It's not much different than that. Let me explain," I said.

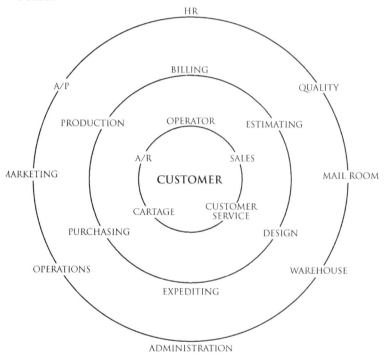

CIRCLES OF SUPPORT
DEPARTMENT CONNECTIONS TO A CUSTOMER

"Rudy and I put the customer in the center of the circles. To use your analogy, Gene, they're like the sun. Every department in the company revolves around the customer, but each at different distances, if you would, from the customer.

"We found that only about a third of the departments come in direct contact with external customers, either in person, by phone or mail. We put these departments in the circle next to the customer. They are sales, customer service, cartage, and accounts receivable. Of course the switchboard operator and receptionist are part of the customer service department.

"The customer contacts those departments with an inquiry, an order, a compliment or complaint. Someone in the department then helps the customer or passes him or her on to be helped by another department in the second circle.

"For example, say a customer calls to check on an order. She talks to the operator first who forwards the call to customer service. A customer service rep then looks up the order and gives the customer the information she needs. That's the end of the transaction.

"But, let's say the customer calls to speak to a sales rep who then takes an order. After taking the order the rep calls it into customer service. Then the order moves on to purchasing and later production. Since the purchasing and production departments don't come in direct contact with a customer they're located in the next circle away from the customer. They don't have direct customer contact. But their product eventually passes back through the inner circle and is delivered to the customer again.

"What about the outermost circle? Some of those departments never deal with a customer's inquiry or order," Carla asked.

"You're right. They don't," I said.

"They support the other departments who take care of customers. What they do has an effect on how everyone else at the company does his or her job.

"An organizational chart shows the chain of command. It shows how a company is structured. This chart has a different purpose. It shows the flow of business through our company and it shows us what our purpose or target is — the customer. All our employees are either next to the customer or one or two steps away from them. It's designed to show how each department relates to a customer."

I thought again about Gene's comment about the solar system and added, "Just like the sun holds the planets in orbit through its gravity, everything we do should gravitate toward a customer. Without the customer we couldn't survive.

"Rudy and I are going to give this chart to management and ask them to replace the pyramid organizational structure. Before we do we wanted your input."

"I like the idea of being in the center of things with administration hanging on the edge. Looks good to me," Naomi blurted out.

"It's not a chart of who is more important; it's not even a hierarchical-type chart at all," Rudy said. "It's purpose is to emphasize that everything we do needs to be customer-centered."

"I like it," said Carla. "Being in purchasing and in the middle I see how what we do can affect the flow of the work process to and from a customer."

"That's what we're after. Thanks for pointing it out," I said.

I put up another overhead.

"This one shows the steps of an individual transaction. It's the linear process of an order. What do you notice about it?" I asked.

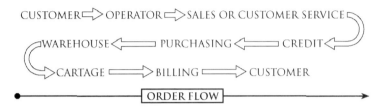

After looking at it a while Brad said, "It begins and ends with the customer. I like it because it represents a continuous flow of work like a running river. Our customers' needs flow through us. It's up to each of us to make everything flow as smoothly as possible. If we do, the customers are likely to send us more orders that'll flow through our system again."

"We also have charts showing each individual department and its work flow," Rudy said. "Put one of those overheads up, Bob."

As soon as I did Naomi asked, "Are we going to see these posted everywhere like the 'We don't need to take care of all our customers, just the ones we want to keep' posters?"

"I hope so," I said.

After a brief discussion it appeared that some people were indifferent about it while some thought it was a good idea. At least no one thought it would cause any harm. The take-care-of-customer posters seemed to create a buzz when they first went up. The whole idea was to get people thinking about the result and purpose of their job.

Later, when I walked into Nancy's office she was on the phone, so I looked around the room while I waited. I noticed several plaques on the wall behind her desk advertising associations we must have belonged to. I wondered if we still did?

"Hi Bob, sorry for the wait," Nancy said as she hung up the phone.

"No problem. Is Allen ready for me?"

"He said you could go on in when you got here."

I walked through his door and saw him at his computer with his back to me. "Hey Allen," I said.

He stopped keying, then spun around in his chair. I could see by the smile on his face that he was in a good mood.

"So, Bob, give me the update on your marketing plan."

"Sure, but I'm curious about what's happening with the Ace Distributor account. Are we going to be able to supply their other locations?"

Dave Hankins was at that moment out of state at Ace's main office. We had been supplying one of their divisions located near us for years. Dave was trying to secure their account nationwide. It would mean a lot of business for us if he did.

"That was his email I was just replying to. Dave said they were open to the idea of consolidating their business with one vendor and had given him all the forms they use at all their facilities. He said he's confident we can combine some of their forms from several locations and eliminate others altogether. By having us run all their forms nationwide they'll gain consistency between their operations, and it'll surely reduce the total dollars they spend by dealing with one supplier instead of several across the country. Dave said it looks like a great opportunity to lock up a lot of business and help Ace at the same time."

"Isn't that the point," I asked, "to serve the customer? The sales rep found more customer wants which will help leverage more profit for us, right?"

"You keep coming back with that fulcrum model, but I guess you're right. It was those SWOT questions he used that opened this opportunity for us." He continued. "I'd never considered location as a marketing decision before, but I can see now that we can't limit our market to how far our delivery trucks go."

"Location isn't where we are. Location is anywhere a customer can be, such as near a phone, the Internet or even a fax machine. Remember when we first started accepting orders via fax? That was a marketing decision."

"So how is your marketing plan coming?" Allen asked.

"Excellent. The feedback that sales is gathering from customers combined with the internal surveys from the employees has helped form the plan. In addition to location, it looks like we've found some opportunities in our pricing and product line, too. The one area we seem to already have well covered is promoting our products through our sales force.

"By the way, I was wondering about the plaques I saw on the wall behind Nancy's desk. Do we belong to all of those associations?"

"Probably not all of them," Allen said. "I get some publications each month so we must be members of at least a few."

"Is anyone from our company going to any of the meetings or involved with them in any way?"

"I don't think so. Why?"

"Well, one of the ways to increase the promotion of our company is through networking. Associations would be a good start, don't you think?"

"Maybe," Allen said with little enthusiasm. "Why don't you find out which ones we belong to and come up with a plan to identify who at our company should be involved with them and how it'll benefit us?"

I wrote it down as a to-do. It was another area to investigate.

Then I showed him the business chart Rudy and I had developed. I wanted Allen to see it before I revealed it at the next management meeting. I wanted his approval first.

He liked it, but felt it would be best to let the managers look at it first and get their feedback before adopting it. After all, it was their privilege to review any company policy changes before they were implemented.

I told Allen that the marketing plan would be completely outlined by the end of the following week. That way the managers would get a chance to review it before the end of the month. I assured him, barring any major changes occurring, that he'd have it completed to submit to Consolidated by the first week of the following month.

He was pleased to hear it was going to be on time. I told him I was hoping to have some numbers by then to show additional sales we had as a result of the plan.

Allen ended our meeting saying how pleased he was with the progress I'd made.

After I left his office I stopped by Nancy's desk to write down the names of the associations on the plaques. I asked her if she knew if we belonged to any. She opened a file showing the ones we were current members of. She handed me the files and I wrote down the information I needed to contact the associations.

I thought about the last seven weeks. It had been an interesting journey. It seemed that after every door I passed through I'd found two more doors to explore. I never realized that marketing touched nearly every-thing we did at the company. Yet a comprehensive plan was coming together and I was getting down to the final touches. The journey was nearing its end.

CHAPTER SEVENTEEN

O ver the past several weeks, the marketing plan had consumed much of my thoughts. Now, I couldn't believe the last game of Josh's football season arrived so soon. His first year had gone by too fast. Thanksgiving was two weeks away.

Amy stayed at a friend's house the night of the game. She'd had enough of football. The cheerleaders might have drawn her there, but not in the damp, cold weather of November. Kate was bundled up for it, but I was so nervous about the game I wouldn't have noticed a blizzard.

The team's season had gone according to their plan—almost. They'd only lost one game all year. The team they were playing had the same record. Whoever won the game would be the league champs. But that wasn't why I was so nervous.

The boy that started ahead of Josh all season broke his leg in the game the week before and was out for the final game. Josh had gone in for him late in a few games when they were ahead so he had some experience, but for the last game he was a starting player. He'd never started before.

The good thing was he'd had a whole week to mentally get ready to start, but he'd be nervous just the same. I wished I were as prepared as he was. Josh would be able to run off any nervousness he had on the field. My nervousness was bottled up inside. I couldn't wait for the game to be over.

"Do you think Josh is warm enough in those short pants?" Kate asked.

"He probably won't even notice the cold. His mind's on the game and the player across from him, I'm sure."

"I hope he does all right."

So did I. I fidgeted in my seat looking for signs that the game would begin.

Finally the players were in position on the field. The crowd stood up for the opening kickoff. Before I knew it the game was over.

"That was the most exciting game I've ever seen, don't you think so honey?" Kate asked as we walked to greet Josh outside the locker room.

I couldn't agree more. Watching my son start his first game put more of an edge on it than I'd expected. I felt like I'd held my breath for the entire game—at least on every play. I was as exhausted as if I'd been out there on the field with him.

"I wonder if they'll take longer than usual getting out of the locker room?" I asked.

"Probably," Kate replied. "I'm sure the coach will

have a lot to say."

All of a sudden I saw Josh rush out of the gym with his uniform still on.

"Wow! Can you believe it?" he yelled as soon as he saw us. "24 to 18; just like we wrote on the board in the meeting room. We beat the Indians. We're the champs!"

"Congratulations son, I couldn't be more proud of you," I said as I wrapped my arms around him.

"The guys decided we wanted to celebrate so we're all going to clean up and go to the pizza shop. Coach said he's buying. I just wanted to let you guys know I won't need a ride home."

"I understand. Don't be too late. I want to hear all about it when you get home. I'll wait up for you," I said.

"Here's some money if you need it, hon," Kate said as she handed him some bills. "We're so proud of you!"

Josh hugged us one more time then ran back into the gym, jumping and yelling as he went. I know how he felt. There's nothing quite like reaching a goal.

The house was quiet. Kate had gone to sleep. Amy was at her friend's house, and I was relaxing in the family room staring at the family pictures on the wall.

I turned the TV off after the news because nothing else was on. I didn't know if I could stay up long enough to see Josh. I was about to fall asleep in the chair when I heard the click of the front door unlock. Then Josh walked into the room.

"So, did you have a good time celebrating?" I asked.

"The best," Josh replied with a huge smile on his face. "I always thought we'd win the league championship, but now that it's happened it doesn't seem real. I can't believe we actually did it."

Josh sat down on the couch across from me telling me all about the victory party.

I asked him how it was starting for a change. He told me it took a while for him to get comfortable about starting the game at the expense of someone else getting hurt. Before the game he said it didn't feel right to him to get to start under those circumstances. But as soon as he made contact on the first play he knew he deserved to be out there on the field.

He said the coach had made a point to talk with him before the game to explain the importance of the role he was playing. The coach assured him that he wasn't replacing the other player with Josh just because the other player was hurt. He trusted Josh to do the job just as well. Being on second team didn't mean he was necessarily second best. All he and the team expected of Josh was for him to give his best. The coach said if he did that he knew he'd get the job done.

As Josh was talking I wondered how much of what the coach had said was true and how much was said to build Josh's confidence. I guess it didn't matter because the result was Josh believed it and then lived up to it.

"That's a wise coach you have. You mentioned back at the school about the score being exactly what you wrote on the board before the game. What was that about?" I asked.

"Before each game in the meeting room coach would write on the wall a list of what could take place in a game. He'd write things like how many yards our running backs would gain, how many first downs we'd get, how many turnovers, things like that. It was always different for each game. Except at the top of the list was the number of yards we were going to average per down, which was always four, and the number of yards we would give up on defense each play, which was two. Then the last thing on the board was always the score.

"We came up with the numbers as a team. Then after each game we'd come in and coach would write down next to our goals the actual numbers from the game we'd just played. This was the first game we predicted the exact score.

"The first few games we came close, then we lost that game to the Cowboys. We were shocked at the numbers. But coach looked at them more closely over the weekend and discovered something interesting.

"Our running game was just as we had planned— 4 yards per carry. But our overall average was down because our passing fell apart that game. Our quarterback got sacked five times. The line wasn't doing its job. That was the first team we'd played that had challenged us like that and showed us a weakness we didn't know we had.

"The next week we went back to the basics on pass blocking and how to adjust for different formations the defense might give us. We still maintained our strength with our running game, but after that week our passing became even stronger.

"Each week coach would go over the numbers with us again to find other weaknesses, and each week we made minor adjustments.

"By the final game we got ourselves so finely tuned

that we hit our numbers exactly!"

Josh's eyes were as wide open as I'd ever seen them. It was like he'd discovered gold. I thought of how Jensen could discover gold as soon as we knew our weaknesses and started to strengthen them.

"Well, I've got to say I was impressed with your coach's methods all year. I'm not surprised you guys became the champs."

"Dad, I'm going to bed now. My mind feels wide awake, but my body's drained."

"I understand. Good night son. I'm very proud of what you've done."

Just as he was about to walk through the door I jumped up and said, "Wait a minute."

Why only tell him how proud I was? I walked over to him and put my arms around him and held him close. He looked at me and smiled, then went upstairs to bed.

I walked through the house to lockup for the night. When I reached to turn off the light in the family room I glanced at the pictures on the wall once more. The newest picture of Josh in his uniform held my gaze.

He didn't stand out in the game tonight, but he sure worked hard all year to help the team win. I realized now that he was always a part of the team, even when he wasn't starting. His hard work helped the other kids become better players, and when the time came for him to play he was prepared. His coach was right. No one on a team should be insignificant. Everyone should be working toward the same goal.

Lying in bed with the lights out I still couldn't rest my brain. I was thinking about my goal. Would we ever get everyone working toward serving customers? I wished business were as simple as freshman football.

CHAPTER EIGHTEEN

It turned out to be a lovely day when Aunt Patsy and Uncle Phillip finally came to visit us. It seemed like it took forever to get our schedules together. Kate was excited; she loved having guests. I looked forward to reacquainting the kids with Patsy and Phillip.

I was nervous the moment the doorbell rang. I shouldn't have been, but I felt like I needed to make a good impression. Kate got the door first. Josh and Amy got there the same time I did. Phillip was holding a bouquet of flowers and Patsy held what I guessed to be a fabulous dessert.

After all the smiles and hugs and comments on how big the kids were, Patsy and Kate headed for the kitchen with the kids following. Phillip and I ended up in the den. It felt good to have him in my home.

"So, how are things going with the marketing plan?" he asked.

"The good news is I finally have a written plan. The better news is there is no bad news."

"Any results yet?"

"I'm a bit surprised, but yes," I said.

I sat down on the couch and motioned for Phillip to sit beside me. I knew it would take some time to tell him all that had happened since our last chat.

"The managers are confident with the plan we've come up with. We may even exceed our new owner's expectations. We're not expecting any explosive sales numbers, but we can see enough of an increase so far that if it holds for most of the coming year we'll definitely surpass last year's performance."

"So what's happened since we talked?" Phillip asked.

So much, I thought. It was hard to decide where to begin.

"Your idea of looking at four areas for a marketing plan gave us a lot to consider. The feedback we got from our initial surveys helped us decide what we needed to do in each one.

"Our sales force started using the SWOT questions with customers. We found out one of our customers has several locations across the country, but only the local one was buying from us. We landed a large chunk of business with all of them by helping them consolidate and standardize their forms."

"That's great," Phillip said. "You're not limiting your location. That was the very thing that turned around one of the companies I bought several years ago. They weren't looking out to the horizon far enough for potential business."

"And we found other opportunities within the area we've already been serving," I added.

"We started a promotion of giving away some

record storage boxes with our name printed on them. It started out as a little extra thing to do when we sent out orders over a certain dollar amount. Our sales reps figured the customers would need to store the forms they bought eventually, so why not give them something to store it in before they needed it. Someone came up with the idea of using the storage boxes to send our products in, but that idea didn't turn out to be very practical. But adding them to orders has worked out great. We've had several customers call us just to order more of the storage boxes."

"Did you sell them the boxes?"

"Yes. Now we stock them in our warehouse as a product and not just a promotion. We still give out some at no-charge depending on how big the order is, but we're actually selling boxes now, too."

"That's why convenience stores are so packed with stuff," Phillip said. "The space is already paid for whether they display something for sale or not. Might as well use that space for something that can help a customer and earn a profit for you."

"We're looking into other items to sell, too," I added. "But we decided that they must do two things. First, the products have to relate to what we already sell. We didn't want to be like a gas station convenience store that sells items unrelated to gas or oil such as sodas and food. We didn't want customers coming to us to buy a few record storage boxes and nothing else. We want to be selling them printed materials along with whatever else we can supply them.

"And second, the items we sell have to be profitable. If it helps our customer at our expense, what's the point?"

"That's a fine line you're walking, Bob. If a customer buys a new item in addition to another one he already buys, you could look at the profitability of the entire order and not that of each item separately. But be careful if customers start ordering only the convenient items without the high profit ones."

"We thought of that. More specifically we decided we'd only add new items if they were profitable by themselves and not items just to leverage profit," I said, rephrasing my original statement.

"That sounds good," Phillip said. "Eventually by becoming more valuable to your customers you'll be able to get a higher margin on your products. People don't mind spending a little more if they get more value in the end."

"That's the result we're looking to create," I said.

"How are the people inside taking all of this? Change can be unsettling when they don't see any tangible rewards for themselves."

"They're taking it amazingly well. I think partly because they've been involved in the changes. Several of the ideas, so far, are from workers in the trenches. Up to now, this hasn't been a management dictate. The employees have bought into the philosophy that they need to improve in order for the company to improve. It's become a job security issue for them.

"I believe the other reason they're taking it so well has to do with the new business chart we came up with. We put a large poster with all the employees' names on it in the sequence that they add value to a customer. The point was to give each worker a clear view of how he or she contributes in relationship to serving a customer.

They can see graphically how they personally add value to the process. And they now understand where their paycheck comes from—the customer.

"So morale is up?" Phillip asked.

"That's the least you could say. And with the surveys we used with our suppliers we've actually found ways to make work easier for them and ourselves. The same has been happening with our internal customers."

I went on telling him how the customer relations department had revised the new job folders and how Carla had eliminated her ordering problems with vendors by getting them to help identify how to describe the material we order to avoid mistakes.

He asked me what customer relations was. He said he'd never heard that term used at a manufacturing company before.

I explained to him our new department names and how each was prefixed with the words customer service since every department ultimately served customers. The idea was to make everyone aware how they're involved in serving customers, even with no direct contact. But then we faced a dilemma as to what to call our old customer service department.

"We came up with customer relations since their job was to take a customer's inquiry and relate it to the company. If it was an order to be entered, they handled it themselves. If it was a follow-up to an order, they contacted the appropriate department and then got the information they needed and related the answer back to the customer. It seemed more accurate, and it implied a higher degree of responsibility, too."

Phillip liked the idea of the entire company being

considered customer service rather than just a few peo-ple in one department.

"Sounds like you've got a firm grip on growing your company," Phillip said.

"It's strange, but just a few months ago I hadn't a clue as to how we were going to increase our market share, and now we have a plan in place, improvements in more areas than we expected, and it looks like we'll have more than enough growth to satisfy Consolidated."

"Is that confidence I hear in your voice?"

"No doubt," I said with pride.

Phillip leaned over to me and put his hand on my shoulder. He paused to gather his words before speaking. I had no idea what he was going to say.

"Bob, I may end up buying a company within the next several weeks. If it comes through I'm going to need someone with your type of insight to help develop it's potential. Do you know anyone you might recommend?"

I took his question seriously and tried to think of someone I knew who could do the job. Then it occurred to me; he was really offering me the job and hoping I'd say that I could do it.

"Are you asking if I would take the job?" I asked.

"Why not? You'd be perfect for it. You'd eventually become a part owner, of course, and would be running it practically by yourself. I'm sure you could do it."

I wasn't prepared to be offered a job. I was startled and unsure of what to say.

"Phillip, I'm very honored you've asked me," I said, stalling to gather my thoughts. "I don't want to say no, but I need to ask for some time to consider it. Is that all right? I don't want you to think I'm being ungrateful by not jumping at your offer."

"I understand. I'd expect you to think about it before making a decision. But I want you to know that I have no doubt in your ability. Let me tell you more about it, then you can take your time and let me know after you've thought it over."

I sat there stunned by his offer as he told me about the company he was about to buy. I flashed back to the rash decision I'd made years ago when I'd left the family business, letting my emotions take over. I didn't want to make the same mistake again. I was sure Phillip understood what was going through my head.

He patted my knee and said, "We can discuss this more later. Think about it. Talk it over with Kate. Call me if you have any questions. In the meantime let's go see what everyone else is up to. Something from the kitchen sure smells good."

So we headed to the kitchen and found Kate, Patsy and the kids laughing about old times.

The rest of the evening was filled with more stories and laughter. It seemed like only minutes had passed instead of hours before the four of us were standing on the porch waving good-bye to Patsy and Phillip.

Josh left to go to a friend's house. Amy disappeared upstairs to her bedroom.

"This was a lovely evening, wasn't it honey?" Kate asked.

"I'm sure glad we finally got together. I know Dad would be pleased."

"What did you and Phillip talk about?" she asked

nonchalantly as we strolled into the kitchen to clean up.

"He wants me to run a company he's buying," I dropped without warning.

"What? What company? Where's it located? What do they do?" she asked with excitement. She deliberately left out the obvious question of how much it paid. I knew she'd expect me to answer it, though.

"Well, he hasn't actually bought it yet, but I'm sure it would be a great opportunity for me to run it, with his guidance of course. I'm sure I'd at least make what I do now with a possibility of becoming an owner in the future."

"When does he need you?"

"I haven't given him an answer yet. I told him I needed to think about it. He still needs to actually buy the company."

"Oh Bob, what do you have to think about? This is an opportunity you deserve. Why shouldn't you take it?"

For the rest of the night we discussed the possibilities. Kate was very supportive of my concerns. I felt some obligation to Jensen if for any reason at least for the opportunities they'd given me over the last 18 years. I hadn't told her yet about what they'd offered me just this week because it was all speculative at the time and not a formal offer.

It turned out that Consolidated liked the marketing plan we'd sent them. They wanted me to work with some of their other companies and develop similar plans for them. Allen had also talked about my becoming a vice president, possibly becoming next in charge to him.

Now there was Phillip's offer of a partnership to run a new company of his. I was faced with more opportunities than I could have imagined. Six months earlier when the company was sold I was wondering how long I'd have a job. Suddenly there I was with several to choose from.

Life has its surprises. You never know what's around the next corner. I thought the previous few months had been trying and I was at a dead-end. Now I was faced with exciting possibilities I never imagined.

EPILOGUE

It's been over a year now. I'm planning on leaving early today so Kate and I can see Josh's first league game. He's on the junior varsity team now starting at right guard. If he has a good year he just might start varsity next year. Lucky for Josh, coach Neilson was promoted to be an assistant varsity coach and head coach of the JV squad. I'm sure that's why Josh's doing so well. He really likes his coach.

Too bad Amy isn't cheering for his team. She's a freshman cheerleader this year. That means Kate and I get to go to two separate games a week—one to see her cheer, and one to see Josh play. It keeps us busy and in touch with the kids so it isn't bad at all, really. Next year she'll get the chance to try out for varsity. We'll see.

I probably wouldn't have been able to see their games if I had accepted Consolidated's offer to work with their other companies. They had this idea of me traveling to a different location for two weeks each month. That would've been too much time away from my family. I know I couldn't have stood that much restaurant food, either, so I told them I couldn't do it.

Instead they worked it out that someone from each company came to Jensen and worked there with me rather than me going to them. So far it's working well. I still do some traveling, but I have the flexibility of scheduling it myself; and not for two weeks at a time.

A benefit to everyone is that I'm learning more by working with different product lines. My unfamiliarity actually gives me an advantage of working with other companies since I have no preconceived ideas about their markets. It also allows me to use the ideas from one company and adapt them to several others. I've revised Jensen's plan twice since working with our sister companies.

I actually work for Consolidated now, as vice president of marketing for manufacturing and distribution—quite a title. It's been working out so far with me having an office here at Jensen, though. I wasn't ready to move to Consolidated's headquarters.

Maybe when the kids are out of high school we'll consider relocating. Kate likes the idea of living somewhere else in the country for a change. But for now we're settled here.

Phillip's offer to run his company fell through—he never bought it. He said the deal turned out to be something other than what he was originally presented. He didn't need the money anyway and it would have interfered with his traveling.

We get together often now. Business inevitably comes up, but our visits are more social—I'm not trying to get business advice anymore. From time to time, though, he asks how things are at Consolidated as if to check and see if I'm available should he come across another business opportunity. If the right one comes up, we'll see. For now I'm happy where I am.

And at Jensen, Rudy Alarcon's going to retire at the end of this year, and he deserves it. Brad was offered his position but declined. I think he turned it down because he has something on the side he's working on, but that's okay. He's better with machinery than people anyway.

It was decided to give Rudy's job to Gene Brooke instead. Since Rudy gave the company six months notice of his retirement it allowed plenty of time to train Gene. It's amazing how he's taken to it. He's much more of a people-person than Rudy was, not that Rudy did a bad job, but Gene's people skills will enable him to do even better things.

Carla loves her job. She set it up so she has more flexibility to take care of her kids. She's happy with where she is. I see her being our purchasing manager for a long time.

And Walter's still here. We thought we'd lose him after all our accounting functions moved to headquarters. Apparently there was an arrangement that insured Walter a job as long as he wanted. Who knew of all the deals that were made when the company was sold? Regardless, the company's back on track with Mr. Jensen's original purpose.

I can still hear his words, "Take care of the customer." We are, and their orders are taking care of profits.

ABOUT THE AUTHOR

Terry L. Mayfield has been a straight-commission salesperson for over 20 years. As Vice President of Sales for a national manufacturer/distributor of packaging products his award-winning career was built on repeat sales that focused on customers' wants and needs. He trains others with his "How to Create the Perfect Customer" and "Selling Through Service" seminars and audiotape programs. He is also the author of the self-help book, *How to Control Your Destiny.* He speaks to corporations and associations across the country on customer service, sales & marketing and personal success and is a professional member of the National Speakers Association.

To book Terry L. Mayfield to speak at your next meeting or conference please call toll-free 1-888-251-5077, or visit http://www.MayfieldTraining.com.